Nathaniel J. Wilson, Ed.D.

ULTIMATE LEADERSHIP

VOLUME 1

The Defining Moment

published by

Reach Worldwide, Inc.
Sacramento, CA

Ultimate Leadership Volume 1: The Defining Moment
by Nathaniel J. Wilson, Ed.D.

© 2003 Reach Worldwide, Inc.
Sacramento, CA

ISBN 0-9717739-1-2

All Scripture quotations in this book are from the King James version of the Bible unless otherwise noted.

Printed in the United States of America
First publication May 2003

Printing and Design Services: 7Dcreative.com

For additional copies contact:
Reach Worldwide, Inc.
P.O. Box 292100, Sacramento, CA 95829
(800) 762-5990
www.reachworldwide.org

Price $14.99

Dedication

To Verbal Bean: Rarely can a leader, virtually single-handedly, and on his own shoulders, revolutionize a people group. He did. He was a member of that small group of the rarest of men. A man of another level. One in a generation—I am glad it was mine.

To Mary Wilson: A woman with crystal clear understanding of feminine ebb and masculine flow, of receiving and returning dreams, of what it means to be one of "two who agree." Thank you and I love you.

Acknowledgements

This book is based on the conviction that leadership greatness is born out of acquaintance with, and individual engagement with life's most primal and powerful forces. Ultimate leadership does not begin with do's and don'ts, but rather with the invisible and the spiritual. It is other-worldly. However (Alas!), we are still in this world and therefore we are dearly dependent upon people blessed with high understanding and skills in the organization and completion of such a task. The skill of these faithful and dedicated people are extensive. They deserve much credit in the completion of this task. They are as follows:

Tara Bollmann for countless, exhausting hours of word processing and repeated generations of corrections and re-writes with never a word of complaint. Certainly my writing often demanded the "gift of interpretation."

Jennifer Butts for proofreading, editing, and special attention to form and style, as well as help with coherence and transitions.

Patricia Bollmann for proofreading, editing, and extensive and repeated assistance in grammar and re-writing for clarity. (Note: Both Jennifer and Patricia suggested some corrections which I did not heed. Therefore, any errors are mine.)

Robert Fuller for his considerable help and suggestions.

The (very precious) Rock Church for allowing me time to write.

Our lovely Lord for the high honor of working with Him.

About the Author

Dr. Nathaniel Wilson is President of the Leadership Institute and bishop of The Rock Church. The Rock Church began with 6 members and has grown to some 1300 members with 6 branch works. A new sanctuary is under construction which will seat up to 5,000. Dr. Wilson has been teaching leadership seminars for many years and is recognized in breakthroughs in Apostolic leadership formation and understanding of effective leadership worldwide. He has authored numerous books including "In Bonds of Love" and "The Defining Moment." He is married and has two daughters, Rebecca, married to Doug Salters, and Sheila, married to Myles Young (all leaders). Myles and Sheila have two children, Boston and London.

Accomplishments include:

- Founder of satellite campus classes of Hope International University (Fullerton, CA) and Patten College (Oakland, CA) in Sacramento, California
- Founder of Reach Satellite Radio Network
- Founder of Leadership Summit, an annual enclave for church and educational leaders.
- Founder of PenteCom, an international radio network and publishing group.
- Co-Founder of "No Limits," a leadership conference for young ministers and evangelists attended by approximately 2,000 annually.
- Founder of Connect Magazine and contributing Editor to World Report, both magazines published internationally for ministers and religious leaders in general.

Table of Contents

A Note from the Author

For the believer, the Kingdom of God is the one enterprise on earth that supersedes all others. It is the only kingdom that deals with issues of ultimacy. It is unique. It does not stand in the list of earth's nations and is not recorded with them. *"He sheweth his word unto Jacob, his statutes and his judgments unto Israel. He hath not dealt so with any nation: and as for his judgments, they have not known them"* (Psalm 147:19, 20). Altogether above and distinct, the church is the point of entry of God into human affairs in a personal and salvific way. This is not true of any other group of people. Thus, the church and its mission hold a place of primacy.

Such a mission is great and universal. If "world-class" leadership is essential in any sphere of human endeavor, it is even more so in the Kingdom of God. This leadership demands penetrating insight, wide-ranging wisdom, deep compassion, and an understanding that hostile, opposing spiritual forces exist. The fact of this hostility requires the leader to be equipped with a knowledge of this opposition as well as how to overcome it. The church deals daily with foundational issues of human existence, the purpose of history and of divine intent. Thus, if "greatness" in leadership is needed anywhere, it is needed in the church. Such greatness is more than the sum total of theological knowledge, vocational skills, and speaking skills. It is more than utilitarian efficiency. There is a deep, radical, powerful enduement and balance in such great leadership. Not many go there. As a result, the true spiritual leaders of the world are but a small band. If the forces of darkness that oppose this band prevail, nothing will remain except the lonely moaning of the wind through the ruins of defeat.

The content of this book is taken from a broader corpus of

material included in a series of graduate courses taught on the subject of "Human Spirituality and World-Class Leadership." The presentation of the content that follows is preceded in the classroom by a relatively large body of other material. However, in regards to actual experience that moves one toward leadership greatness, the content of this book definitely holds primacy of position and is therefore the first to go to print. Further, while many of the principles found herein are applicable to a wide range of leadership venues, the primary intent of this volume is to provide direction for leadership development in the most critical and seminal area of all, that is, leadership in spiritual ministry. Paul informs us that we have been given a "ministry of reconciliation," a mandate to proclaim a message of hope and to lead those interested to reconciliation with God. What a charge! Standing between two worlds, the reconciling leader has the highest of all leadership challenges.

The plan is to develop the entire body of materials that make up the foundation of the leadership teachings in the classroom courses. It is our hope to quickly follow with the publication of the second volume in this series. Following is a brief outline of the progression from beginning formation for leadership to the final goal of leadership training.

What is the final goal of leadership training? The answer is simple. It is effective

Figure 1

Because effective ACTION is the final goal of any leadership training, focus is usually placed here. The desired result of this ACTION is to lead others to goals beneficial to each follower as well as to the goals of the leader. That is what leadership is about. However, effective ACTION is seldom achieved by a myopic focus on action itself.

ACTION alone does not contain within itself the answers needed to produce sustained effectiveness. For action to be effective, it must be empowered by precedents to action. Many have exhausted themselves by attempting, through ACTION alone, to achieve satisfactory results. Frustration and exhaustion eventually culminate in a relinquishing of one's hoped for outcomes and in an eroding of one's goals until mediocrity finally becomes acceptable.

So what must precede ACTION to make it more effective? Why do some work harder than others with far less results? What did Jesus mean when He instructed us to "consider the lily," which toils not, yet Solomon in all of his glory was not arrayed like one of these? A microscopic examination of the shiniest gates of Solomon's Temple would reveal thousands upon thousands of small imperfections and scratches. In contrast, the closer one inspects the lily, the more one would discover the incredible order and perfection within. Quantum studies now reveal that, no matter how powerful the microscope, the closer one observes the lily's patterns, the more its beauty self-repeats in an apparently unending and ever smaller repetition. Further, the lily does this by simply *aligning* itself vertically with its source and growing upward while sinking its roots downward into the earth's nutrients. At the same time, it keeps itself in *rhythm* with the light, receiving life through the cyclical rhythm of the sun. In the same sense, the subjects which we believe are essential to a firm understanding of spiritual enablement for leadership include such revelatory truths—truths that derive squarely from scripture, but that often require more than surface reading to discover. In order to ferret out the essential truths needed to inform ACTION, the whole corpus of a specific subject must be pondered before arriving at in-depth conclusions. Thus, as shown in the brief figure below, to have effective ACTION, one must "go backward" before going forward. An understanding of PROGRAM (organization) is essential if there is to be sustained, effective ACTION. Obviously, ACTION that is not informed by a plan and that lacks order and sequence will soon become confusing and wasteful and will eventually come to either mass confusion or to a complete halt. ACTION requires a program.

Figure 2

Because ACTION requires planning and sequencing, we have organizations. The very name "organization" is self-defining. Its purpose, whether a simple plan for some small endeavor or a worldwide strategy enacted to reach a global goal, is the same—that is, to provide some method for insuring that ACTIONS will result in predetermined outcomes. As the size of the desired goal grows, the size of the organization and program need to grow. For example, to reach the entire world with the message of Jesus Christ, and then to maintain and nurture the gains made, men and women organize themselves to avoid wasted repetition and to insure maximum results. Thus, organization is essential for sustained success in realizing desired outcomes.

However, PROGRAM by itself is not enough. PROGRAM (organization), when left to itself without grounding in that which precedes it in theological order, results in self-perpetuation as its primary goal. Lacking a theology of MISSION to guide it, it turns inward, fixating on self-survival as the central mission. This is why an authentic "Mission Statement" is central to the success of any organization, religious or otherwise. Fixation on self-survival results in loss of direction and purpose. Thus, ACTION requires PROGRAM, and PROGRAM requires a theology of MISSION.

Figure 3

MISSION provides boundaries and direction for PROGRAM, which, in turn, provides guidance for ACTION, which hopefully results in desired outcomes. However, as is the case with ACTION and PROGRAM, MISSION is not sufficient to be the beginning motivational force for sustained effectiveness in leadership. MISSION, unless it is informed by something broader, something deeper, something stronger, will also fail in seeking to become the foundation for great leadership action. Even more shocking is the fact that, unless mission is informed and mediated by something beyond itself, it produces killers. For example, long before he led the Hebrew people out of Egypt, Moses understood that it was God's will for them to be free of Egyptian rule. He prematurely attempted to begin the MISSION of deliverance without sufficient understanding and preparation. His fragmentary understanding of MISSION caused him to develop a defective plan (PROGRAM) for effecting the MISSION. He then took ACTION by taking an Egyptian's life! However, because his actions were not rooted in something deeper than MISSION, they were disastrous. Rather than producing liberation, he produced confusion. Both his timing and methods were erroneous. Evidently having some idea of his purpose, he took action. The result was death. The very people he was destined to lead now saw him as a threat rather than a savior. He lost his position and was forced to flee to the desert. All appeared lost. While Moses apparently understood his mission, at least partially, he wasn't ready for such a mandate. Therefore, MISSION, uninformed by something deeper, produces death and destruction.

New Testament leadership also reveals this need for something deeper than MISSION. Saul, who became Paul, repeated Moses' mistake. Before his encounter with God on the road to Damascus, Paul understood that God had a MISSION. He deeply immersed himself in the carrying out of his understanding of MISSION. However, though we was very intelligent, highly educated, and highly regarded, he did not know what he thought he knew. He was, like Moses, woefully ignorant of the divine requirements for effective ministry. He wreaked havoc and confusion, which eventually resulted in the murder of Stephen. Immersion in MISSION was not enough. The pattern in scripture is that one is never ready for MISSION until one first experiences divine VISION. Both Moses (at the burning bush) and Paul (on the road to Damascus) had to learn this hard lesson before attaining their highest leadership effectiveness. MISSION is shaped by and emerges from divine VISION.

Figure 4

There is so much to be said about the broad subject of spiritual formation. However, for now, the focus of this monograph is the "defining moment" of spiritual formation. There is a "primary spiritual event instant," which becomes the foundation and wellspring for all else. By use of the words "moment" and "instant" we do not mean that this initial formation experience is completed in 60 seconds. The meaning is rather that it is a well-defined impress in a relatively short period of time of one's life in which the individual is forever marked and that guides all succeeding actions.

The core message of this book revolves around the fact that this "defining moment," this "primary spiritual event instant," is that from which great ministry is derived. The phrase "primary spiritual event instant" is defined as follows:

Primary - There are many spiritual events in the life of a leader. However, the premise of this book is that all great ministry derives from one such event in the individual's life that is above all others (i.e., primary). This event may not be the first spiritual encounter of the leader, chronologically speaking, but it is unquestionably primary in terms of importance.

Spiritual - In the context of this lesson, "spiritual" means an encounter with God. It is authentically transcendent. It is unconnected to frivolous curiosity or other such human claims to spiritual experience. Due to its nature, it is experienced only by those "in Christ." It is Christ Himself revealing His claim and call to His leader. Engaging all three domains of man (cognitive, affective, skills) one is transported to a deeper arena of life in which the curtain is parted and one is left standing on the precipice of the cosmic and the universal. Returning from such, one is never the same. While ministry may be somewhat effective without such an experience, no world-class, great leadership can develop in a ministry that lacks it.

Event - The use of the term "event" simply means it is a real life-changing, many-faceted occurrence. It is an epiphany. It is cathartic yet instructive and empowering.

Instant - The use of "instant" here is not meant to designate minutes or seconds. Rather, this primary event may continue for a number of days or even weeks (e.g., Jesus, 40 days or longer). However, when viewed from within the individual who has experienced the event and in comparison to the whole of the rest of one's life, it appears as an instant of revelation and empowerment that informs one's ACTION with supernatural effectiveness. This primary spiritual event instant is not experienced under ACTION or PROGRAM or MISSION, but goes beyond all of these to VISION. It is a visionary experience.

Thus, VISION comes very close to the taproot of effective leadership. As shown in Isaiah's vision of the Lord (chapter 6), there are three movements in the visionary experience. The third movement in vision gives one a vison of the task or mission (verse 8). The second movement gives a vision of self (verse 5). The first movement gives one a vision of God (verse 1). It is in this vision of God that spiritual formation begins and a Theology of Spiritual Formation is developed.

Figure 5

This completes the leadership development vinculum. In the college classroom, the above material, along with collateral courses, comprises a graduate course in Human Spirituality and Leadership. The book you are about to read is located in Section 7 (of 8) in the first of the five divisions expressed above. The whole is entitled Toward Theology of Spiritual Formation. Our plan is to complete, in successive volumes, a series that will include all that is shown in figure 5 above.

The desired result of this work is to produce leaders who, beginning with Spiritual Formation, reverse the arrows in Figure 5 above, culminating in effective ACTION, which will impact our world with spiritual change. It is our conviction that Figure 6 below displays a correct path to robust and solid spiritual leadership capable of sustained and ongoing effectiveness on any level of true spiritual world-class greatness.

Figure 6

The purpose of this book is to hopefully open, at least briefly, a window whereby the reader can view the possibility of spiritual greatness on an unprecedented scale. The Kingdom waits for such leaders.

Chapter 1

How Does Spiritual Formation Come?

S piritual formation–is it kairological or chronological? Is it a process, or is it a life-changing instant? An epiphany or plodding development? Is it the result of many sequential steps, of blocks of understanding laid layer upon methodical layer, or is it a divine interruption to one's life, an event that intersects one's historical existence, and does so with a fury that violates all past understandings, present activities, and future plans? Or does spiritual formation come both ways, and if so, does one precede the other, and, if one is intended to precede the other, which comes first and what happens if this precedence is not maintained? The answers to these questions are germane to the whole enterprise of leadership in the days in which we live and lead.

The position of this book is that individual spiritual formation is first the result of a "primary spiritual event instant." Scripture seems to reveal that there is such a distinct event, a happening, an interruption, a breaking-in upon a person. Later, there may be other event instants. Between these, the event instant is "processed." Thus "process" is indeed included in spiritual formation but only as a spillover of these initial "spiritual event instants." When spiritual formation is attempted by process only (i.e., a methodical, vocation-oriented approach), spiritual technicians may result, but such an approach does not produce authentic spiritual formation, nor does it provide the seedbed for spiritual greatness. Thus, the question of how spiritual formation breaks into one's historic existence is critical to this subject and is tied directly to the larger question of how the Kingdom of God comes to the earth.

It is natural to think of human history as a line of time (Gr. kronos) running horizontally. This time line is divided into seconds, minutes, hours, days, etc. Eventually, the line runs into centuries. History is perceived as ticking by, second by second. This method of viewing history is chronological. It is organized around the familiar predictability of the clock (i.e., "chronometer"). This predictability brings comfort because it leads us to believe that the future will also be comprised of minutes, hours, days, etc. Because of this men are able to plan and to schedule. Patterns are established. These repeatable methods lead to the effective formation of a society. In business, based on this dependable line of "time," these repeatable methods become "business practices." In development of family and time-based religious and societal practices, this development is called "traditions." As a group of people figures out how to live together, this development is called "culture." This culture, extended over a period of years, creates what we call a "history." Using the reliability and dependability of time as a foundation, people find identity through the development of shared practices, traditions, culture, and history.

People groups, whether political, national, racial, or religious, come to possess a shared history. Not only is this history shared, but through time, emotional attachments are created. This shared history comes to be embraced, protected, and defended by its participants. Interruptions to this flow are viewed as threats to the continuation of the group's values and traditions and are usually resisted vigorously.

Earlier we observed that a people group's history, when viewed chronologically, is conceived of as a horizontal line. However, there are many people groups, and each has its own historical time line. Each group carries with it a set of values, practices, traditions, and culture. In turn, each group embraces its own familiar, comfortable line and stands ready to defend it. However, even though all these lines run in the same general direction, they unfortunately do not run perfectly parallel. Rather, they bump into and criss-cross one another to varying degrees. The time-line of one group may go far before crossing another, ever drawing closer to conflict. Even though both may continue in the same general direction, they eventually conflict. The result is war. Each group struggles to maintain its own familiar and cherished practices, traditions, and culture. However, as a result of this "bumping," adjusted values, traditions, and culture emerge over time. We have a "world history" of such conflict, change, and readjustment as history moves along from the past, through the present, and to the future. Herein one group will move alongside another group as they both move through time. New kingdoms arise through intrigue, assault, or assimilation. Leaders arise one day only to be toppled the next. Kingdoms continue to rise and fall. All of this takes place on the "train called time" as it continues to chug on interminably from the past, through the present, to the future. All human kingdoms belong to this realm called time and all trudge together out of the pact, clutching the familiar as they move uncertainly into the future.

How does the Kingdom of God break into such an earth? Does it merge and emerge as all other kingdoms? Or does it come vertically and intersect human history? How does it enter into this flow of human history? At the beginning of His ministry, Jesus declared, "the time is fulfilled, the Kingdom of God is at hand." When He made this declaration, there were numerous views of how the Kingdom of God would come to the earth. This has not changed. Today there remains a variety of such views.

For example, several years ago a group of Catholic priests from Europe exported the idea of "Liberation Theology," their version of how the Kingdom of God makes entrance into earth life. Observing places like Central and South America, they saw oppression of the poor by wealthy landowners and corrupt politicians. They concluded that the poor were justified in using physical violence and military force to overthrow the rich and the powerful. Therefore, since ideas do have consequences, they supported revolutionaries such as Che Guevara and others, who attempted the violent overthrow of these governments. They did this in the apparently sincere belief that this was the method by which justice and the Kingdom of God could come to the earth. In this way, they developed their own version of a sort of apocalyptic entrance of the Kingdom of God into the earth.

Another example has arisen out of "mainline" Protestantism. This idea is called "Reconstructionism." Central to this concept is the teaching that the moral law of the Old Testament should be revived and be the unbending cornerstone of human government. In contrast to the apocalyptic tradition, this view teaches that this should be instituted gradually. The Kingdom of God will slowly infiltrate civil government, incrementally moving it towards becoming the Kingdom of God. This teaching has gained a surprising number of adherents even though it is taught that this coming of the Kingdom will be very gradual—in fact, so gradual that some of the main exponents of this notion estimate that it will take approximately 33,000 years to bring it to pass!

Not to be left out, numerous Charismatics have adopted still another very old concept concerning the coming of the reign of God's Kingdom into human society. Making adaptations to fit their theology, they have embraced "Dominion Theology," or "Kingdom Now" theology. This view sees the Kingdom of God becoming concrete in the earth and overtaking human government through a spiritual revival and renewal. Revival will sweep America and the world with politicians being converted, or else believers being elected to take their place in office, thus ushering in the Kingdom of God through spiritual renewal leading to political dominion.

The above are sincere, howbeit misguided, notions produced or adapted in the 20th century regarding the establishment of the reign of God's Kingdom in the earth. However, such attempts actually go back much farther with tentacles that reach deep into history, tentacles that lead to sobering, and sometimes frightening outcomes. An example of this type of doctrine, which numerous countries have adopted and adapted through the years, derives from the Church of England, or Anglican Church. The idea is that their specific nation is actually "Old Testament Israel," and they are "the elect people of God," "the true Jews," who are the literal descendants of Abraham. If this is true, of course, it provides them with a special position among nations and makes their homeland the special "land of God" from which the rule of the Kingdom of God will be imposed upon the world. Perhaps the most pronounced and deeply entrenched form of this is called "British Israelism."

"British Israelism" is the doctrine that England, and the English people, are literally the true nation of Israel, and that the descendants of Ephraim and Manasseh are the United States and England. This is a national doctrine in England, and is clearly foundational to the theology of the Church of England. In contrast to the United States, the Church of England is the church of the state. Rather than separation of church and state, the state is, doctrinally, considered to simply be the church doing the business of ruling the land, and in the days of the glory of the British Empire, ruling much of the world. Westminster Abbey, the main state church edifice, is located directly across the street from Parliament, and is the final resting place of many of England's great national heroes. Each end of the building contains a massive stained-glass window, one depicting the twelve tribes of Israel and the other depicting the twelve apostles, both representing the idea that, in England, the two have met and are one, that one being the church and nation of England. In the midst of the edifice sits the throne upon which each new king or queen of England has been crowned for hundreds of years. Why is the throne in the church? Because the nation is thought to be God's Kingdom on earth, both Old Testament Israel and the New Testament church. Under this throne is a stone which is dubbed the "Coronation Stone." Their doctrine states that this stone is the literal stone upon which kings of ancient Israel allegedly knelt during their coronation ceremonies. How did the stone end up in England? In the 6th century B.C., during Israel's period of exile, Jeremiah and Baruch transported the stone to England, which made it the new "Israel of God." This doctrine is deeply ingrained nationally in England and Ireland and is embraced not only by members of the Church of England, but also by others who name the Name of Christ in those countries, including Pentecostals and many other faith traditions.

Such a doctrine, if it were true, gives preeminence to the particular nation, lending a sense of sacredness to its land and to its identity. Defending the country then becomes more than patriotism and is elevated to the status of a sacred trust committed to its citizens to defend "God's Kingdom."

The doctrine of British Israelism does not stop there. We have already mentioned that not only is England such, but the United States, as a "brother" to England, is also the home of "true Jews." Consequently, the soil of the U.S. is, in fact, God's nation, Israel, given to the European peoples who colonized the nation 400 years ago. It is, therefore, to be "defended" against "intruders" and "heathens." Every citizen of this, God's holy nation, has a God-given obligation to defend it from infiltration by other ethnic people groups who are not of European stock, and who are thus not the people of God. Some form of this theological belief lies at the core of most of America's militia groups, including the Ku Klux Klan, the Aryan Nation, the "Christian Nation," white supremacists, etc., and reveals the reason for their bigotry, racism, and hatred of immigrants who are not of European heritage.

Such nationalism also reveals a flagrant disregard for any American government that does not protect the nation from immigration and preserve it for "God's people." In such beliefs, it is but a very short step between this elitist belief in one's supremacy and taking up arms to defend one's "holy" country from the "anti-Christ infidels in Washington, D.C." Further, exponents of this belief consider America's churches to be totally bereft of understanding of such matters and completely reprobate concerning these supposed "truths." As a result, these "believers" have utterly no regard for any of the forms of authority in the nation, whether governmental, business, or religious, and proceed to establish their own military groups and "government" compounds. That such beliefs have consequences can be seen in the catastrophic results with groups such as the Branch Davidians in Waco, Texas, the loss of scores of lives in the bombing of the Oklahoma Federal Building, the aborted attempt to blow up two of the largest propane tanks in the Western United States in Elk Grove, California, and the mass suicide deaths of the "Heaven's Gate" group in San Diego, California.

The above examples should make it very clear that answering the question of how the Kingdom of God enters into human society carries with it the most serious of consequences. It is a question that demands an answer, however, all attempts to provide the answer through appropriating such identity to any national or ethnic group, regardless of color or century (and many nations and ethnic groups of virtually every hue and color have attempted to do so at one time or another), simply lead to further confusion and devastation.

The truth is that, according to scripture, it is not God's intention to, at this time, usher in the Kingdom of God in a political or national form. The Kingdom of God is, in this age, characterized by hiddenness. How the Kingdom of God comes into the world during the Church Age is perhaps most clearly revealed in Matthew 13. In each of the seven examples found there, it is clear that the Kingdom presently comes into the affairs of men by entrance into individual human hearts in a spiritually salvific way. It comes silently, submerged from the sight of men, growing unthreateningly within individual hearts.

However, this coming of the Kingdom of God into each human heart occurs in precisely the same apocalyptic way in which the Kingdom of God is predicted to come in its future, universal, political form on the earth. Thus, each individual conversion becomes a micro-cosmic "sign" to the present world of how the Kingdom of God will eventually arrive in its macro-cosmic coming. Following conversion, the new life of each converted individual becomes a witness, a statement to the world, of what life on earth looks like where the Kingdom of God reigns.

Here are common human beings, living life in the common human way, day after day, scheduling, planning, and attempting to gradually make progress. The convert candidates are simply living life, going to school or work, developing relationships, and methodically planning for the future. Suddenly, they somehow are confronted by the claims of the gospel. They are exposed to the manifest power of God. God calls them, tugs at them, shines His love upon them. However one describes it, it does happen and has happened millions of times. Such ones genuinely are gripped by a divine call. In ways that leave friends and family wondering in awe, the called ones are as ones struck from above. Arrested by a divine draw, they arrive, make their way to an altar, and surrender to Jesus Christ. They are struck so deeply that their lives are interrupted and intersected so violently and with such fury as to leave them willing to literally lose everything precious to them to obtain Him. Such is His power, such is His call. It interferes with past understandings. It disrupts present endeavors. It changes future plans. Oftentimes, it violates family, friends, spouse, employer, and peers. Like a bomb dropped into a caravan of ants lumbering along down the time line of history, the explosion is every bit as disruptive. It is a visitation from outer space. The results of such visitations are intoxicatingly powerful to the recipient, but often totally misunderstood by and inconsiderate of those nearby. The divine claim on the human soul is so intense that nothing can stand in its way. God becomes an unapologetic violator of the flow of human history, including all of its traditions, culture, and familial and domestic connections. These divine break-ins are utterly overwhelming and usually without any attempt by God to justify the claim to what He considers His. *"The kingdom of heaven suffereth violence, and the violent take it by force"* (Matthew 11:12) and *"...the kingdom of God is preached, and every man presseth into it"* (Luke 16:16). In other words, "kingdom of heaven suffereth violators and the violators take it by force." Who are these that take the Kingdom and what are they violating? They are those who respond to God's call, and consequently violate the expectations and demands of this world so as to make God's demands first and foremost. They are violating this world "system." Only those willing to do so can grasp the Kingdom. They do so with utter abandon. They "press" their way into it at all costs and in disregard to all other voices. There is no compromise, no middle-ground, no negotiating. It is all or nothing.

As a result, spiritual formation does not begin with, nor can it survive in, a detached air of observation. It does not begin with objective and aloof investigation. It is, rather, a subjectively experienced explosion that blasts everything else into oblivion. It is an epiphany, a conversion experience. The widely-known mental powers and single-minded stubbornness of Saul/Paul did not matter, for this experience far transcended all such human determination and easily overwhelmed this stubborn man, leaving him lying in the dust of the road bewildered and bedazzled under the power of the heavenly vision. This, then, is the beginning of authentic spiritual formation.

The scriptural pattern for this divine, kairological interruption of human life can be seen on the birthday of the Church in Acts 2. The biblical description makes it obvious that these first believers received an experience that was other-wordly and powerfully transforming. Power comes with baptism and the infilling of the Spirit, and this occurrence, at first simultaneously experienced salvifically as well as for enduement for service, is oft repeated as God lays His call upon one for specific ministry. While this kairological visitation is utterly transforming, it is not the last such visit to those who are called to specific ministry.

Chapter 2

The Sailor and the Sea

reat leadership is both an art and a science. It deals in abstracts, ambiguities, wisdom, understanding, and knowledge. It is spiritual, complex, multi-layered, and cannot be quantified. It cannot be attained by simply reading a book such as this one. Still, this book can point at, gesture towards, and inspire. To get a grasp of the subject, every available linguistic device is needed. Jesus, knowing full well the limits of "plain language," also readily used a wide range of poetic word tools to articulate His message, including parables, similes, metaphors, and symbols, as well as plain, straightforward statements.

Someone has said that the words "poet" and "prophet" derive from the same root. Holy Writ is filled with both. Proof of this may be found in observation of writings like the following one, rather than in etymology. Such writings merit slow and careful reading, and time should be allotted for reflection. Secular or religious, it would be difficult to find a more prophetic description of the voyage to effective, spiritual leadership than that of the poet/prophet David who describes it as follows:

> *"They that go down to the sea in ships, that do business in great waters; These see the works of the Lord, and his wonders in the deep. For he commandeth, and raiseth the stormy wind, which lifteth up the waves thereof. They mount up to the heaven, they go down*

again to the depths: their soul is melted because of trouble. They reel to and fro, and stagger like a drunken man, and are at their wit's end. Then they cry unto the Lord in their trouble, and He bringeth them out of their distresses. He maketh the storm a calm, so that the waves thereof are still. Then are they glad because they be quiet; so He bringeth them unto their desired haven."   Psalm 107:23-30

There will always be a place for "land travel" images to reveal important aspects of living. However, in the postmodern era in which we live, "sea faring" images are much more applicable. Land travel has guides. Sea travel has navigators. Land travel is a journey. Sea travel is a voyage. Land travel uses maps. Sea travel uses charts. For thousands of years, these charts were fragmentary at best. They didn't show everything because the makers didn't know everything. They gave general directions, identified outstanding landmarks that one would surely see if they were, indeed, on the correct course, and told of known pitfalls to avoid. At best, they were incomplete. However, it was all they had. When the chart makers reached the limits of the known, they wrote, "Beyond here lie dragons." Today we smile at such. However, such descriptions, when applied to the journey to spiritual formation, may be more correct than we have realized before. Beyond the chart, one could rely only on the heavenly direction of the stars. The unaltering spheres of light, though far away, were dependable. But again, one had to know how to read them and couple the alignment of the heavens with the rhythm of the sea. Alignment and rhythm—two important concepts for genuine leadership—are the core components of ministry.

This book is about the voyage to effective ultimate leadership. It is based on three assumptions which should be understood before reading further.

The first assumption is that you, the reader, are deeply interested in taking the journey to unfulfilled visions. You have grown restless and discontent with yourself. You are consumed with a burning passion to bring your visions "to port," that is, to reality. You are thankful for the goals you have reached but you are not satisfied. You see things that you know are supposed to be yours, but are not. You have a dread of letting time compromise God's promises to you, for you sense that with every compromise, a little more of your person dies and survival takes precedence over "becoming." The leveling effect of constant engagement with the mundane gradually erodes glorious dreams, eventually leading to resignation and acceptance of the status quo.

The second assumption is that your dissatisfaction with present progress in achieving life's visions has reached a "boiling point." You are not far from desperation. Previous fears are falling away as frustration emboldens you. You have realized that you are not even close to your potential. Wanting your life to count, you are at the point of being ready to do whatever it takes to get to the next level.

Some 25 years ago, I talked to a noted leader. He was a state leader of many ministers, as well as a civil judge in the county where he resided. Highly educated, very intelligent, and having a wonderful family, he would have been counted as a success by almost any standard. Yet, I will never forget the day that just the two of us sat together in a restaurant. I was about 28 years old at the time. With a wistful gaze, he said something like this: "Son, I am 55 years old. By most standards I am considered successful. But the truth is, I don't feel like I've ever really gotten untracked. I mean *really* untracked." Five years later, he was dead. But not his words. They live on in me. I will never forget them. As I write this, I am 55 years of age. He deepened my resolve not to die having failed to get "untracked."

The Voyage
The Challenge of Departure

It has already been mentioned above that this book is based on three assumptions. Two of them have already been stated. The third assumption is, indeed, a big one. This assumption is that the reader is ready to take the voyage. For several reasons, a little caution may be in order before enthusiastically saying, "Yes!" First, to "go" means accepting the fact that one must "leave." To get somewhere means leaving somewhere. This first principle, though it sounds simple, is not. Much is involved in the fact that arriving entails leaving. One cannot go and stay. It is either the one or the other. Getting "there" means leaving "here." No departure means no arrival–and departure is not easy. Those who depart "do business in great waters" and "see the works of the Lord, and His wonders in the deep." But the mysterious "deep" and "great waters" are far from shore, from home, from the familiar. The wonders are in the deep. *Only in the deep.* There are no wonders for those remaining on land, or in the wading pool, or by the babbling brook. One can go in the wrong direction in the deep and become lost on some remote horizon. Nevertheless, to the deep we must go.

Nests of familiarity produce comfort levels that are extremely difficult from which to pull away. The pull of the known, of the habitual, of the familiar, must be broken. People misunderstand. Friends object. Loved ones fear. Careful ones caution. Doomsdayers warn. Status-quo resists. Tears and terror block the way. Biological ligatures of love, relationship, and possessions feel the tearing and ripping which result from the inexorable call to the deep. Fear reigns at the sight of the small, very vulnerable ship in the very deep, foreboding water covered in the mysterious dark of night. Many claim they are going. Still others think they will. But when the time arrives, most don't and won't. Only a few truly board. Of the rest, their vision will be filed down by the entrapment of the familiar and ultimately succumb to the many forces that resist the vision. Minutiae and the mundane will rule the day, preventing confrontation with the deep. The start stops most.

The Challenge of Adjustment to a Fluid World

Further hesitation arises upon discovery of the type of voyage being undertaken. According to the psalmist, the leaving whereof we speak is not a cross-country excursion, nor is it a trek or march across land. There is no road! One will miss the reassuring "thunk" of feet on solid ground and the predictability of step after methodical step, and all is given up for the awareness of being surrounded by others, by villages, towns, and cities. It is a fluid world where navigation is required. It is a sea voyage, a journey through deep, tumultuous waters. Indeed, it is a journey, but a water journey. One cannot "cut a trail," because water doesn't cut. There are no trees to blaze. Leaving the firm and seemingly sure surfaces of life, one boards the rocking ship and comes to know and live in the liquid, ever-rocking, ever-changing world of faith. It is the world of the sailor, the world of those called to lead, a rolling deck where endless readjustment is the price of balance and survival.

The psalmist thus portrays his leadership message in nautical images. These are appropriate for our time and place. Land-based images may aptly describe the journey to successful leadership in other venues, but the poet demonstrates that the present-day journey to successful ministry and leadership must be described with sea-based images. Whereas modern society's definition of God has Him "docked," (e.g., "**ground** of being") (Sweet, 1999), navigating in our post-modern society is definitely fluid.

As a result, the surfaces in this post-modern era are not

landscapes but seascapes, with the waters always shifting and the surface never the same. The chaotic sea defies boundaries. It is no accident that "chaos" has become a primary word in our day. Neither is it accidental that Genesis, as we shall see, begins with an unmistakable connection of the ideas of chaos and water. While fixity often seems preferable, fluidity is the reality (ibid.).

Journeying in water connects us with both the days of the psalmist and the first century church whose symbols (fish and boat) were also aquatic. Christ accomplished much of His ministry on or around water. The didactic content of numerous miracles reveals victorious life in a liquid world. First century Palestine was not only shored by the Mediterranean and watered by Galilee, but was well acquainted with aquatic metaphors in its religious life. The loaves of bread offered in the Jerusalem Temple were in the form of a dancing ship, and the ladle used to draw wine from the jug in the Temple had the shape of a ship floating in the sea. Further, eight of the disciples were fishermen and three came from "Beth-sayda," or the "house of fishing" (Patai, 1998). Water images thus tightly link today's ministry with scripture and first century Christianity.

It's About Business

The voyage is a business trip, not a pleasure cruise. It is only for those who will "do business." There is no business more serious, no success more important, no failure with consequences more far-reaching, than eternal business. Success will require learning and patience and endless attention to detail. It will entail proficiency not only in sailing but also in business, investing, protecting, and profit-taking. Sailors? Yes, but also stewards of the "mysteries of God" (1 Corinthians 4:1). Not so fearful as to refuse to invest, and therefore have no profit, yet not so careless as to lose the initial investment unwisely. *"Cast thy bread upon the waters: for thou shalt find it after many days,"* says the wise man. How does one do this? Is the writer saying to stand on the shore and throw pieces of bread into the water? Obviously not. What he is saying is, "Load your grain (as a true visionary, he sees the grain already in its final state, as "bread") in ships and take it to markets having no grain, thus insuring a much better price." Distance from ready availability of the basic staple creates value. It is the old law of supply and demand. Making "safe" plans that transfer the grain to the nearest neighbor, who has easy access to other sources, is easier and much less risky, but brings little profit. Great plans, in contrast, demand great thoughts, great risks, great ventures. They demand expansion, frustration, discomfort, and changes. Everybody cannot do it. Everybody will not do it. Maybe everybody should not do it (we are not sure about that). But you are not "everybody," and God has laid His hand on you, and it is becoming increasingly heavy. Caught by God between "the edge" and "the familiar," you are teetering on the precipice of destiny's call. You are not the first. Others before you have walked there. Nevertheless, there is no escaping the fact that *each must go alone.* By yourself you enter. Passing through the threshold, you plunge into a world that will alter you forever. Development of greatness requires meeting the challenge of great waters.

Going Deeper

Why do business in "great waters" or "the deep"? Obviously, many are not going to do so. Nevertheless, this is where one can "see the works of the Lord, and His wonders in the deep." These wonders are seen only in the deep. There is no other way.

Not many make the trip. When discussing such a treacherous journey, one will hear much about "staying balanced." What is often meant by "balance" is to stay on dry land. Or, if one insists on entering the water, then he or she will be cautioned to stay safely in the shallows and not go out too far. Stay away from the sailors. Stay away from the big ships. Stay out of the deep. Be careful not to let them influence you. No risk. No great waters. No powerful current. No great business, and, consequently, no great wonders.

So what should you do? *"Launch out into the deep!"* encourages Christ (Luke 5:4). "Launch!" The word is an action verb. Getting on board demands risk. At some point, one must act to get on board. It entails leaving the old and stepping toward the new. Leap on or "walk the plank" to get on. Either way, the hard surface and security of the dry land is left behind. Strait is the plank and narrow is the way on board. The ship is made for the deep. It is not the way of the fearful, the conservative, the cowering. However, it is God's way.

> *"Thy way is in the sea, and thy path in the great waters..."*　　　　　　　　Psalm 77:19

Several years ago, a very sincere young minister visited our home. He came into my office where I was working. I invited him to sit down, and we engaged in small talk. After awhile he said, "Talk to me. Tell me something that will help me to be effective and to improve my ministry." At his request, I introduced him to a chain of four or five connected subjects that I considered important to advanced ministry and leadership. I explained that the subject was much bigger than the few minutes we had there in the office. He was obviously interested and listened attentively as I briefly outlined the primary points. After ten or fifteen minutes, he was strongly impacted with the subject matter. Then, after a pause, he asked, "Do you have this in some kind of short sound bites that I could just assimilate in a few seconds?" Rather than reveal my true feelings, I simply made a casual gesture and waved away the conversation by saying, "Hey, let's go get a Coke."

The above scenario is not unusual. I get many such requests. "Do you have this in an outline form?" Or, "I like this. Is it on tape somewhere that I can just listen to it?" While these requests, I suppose, do have some merit, the real truth is that greatness isn't packaged in sound bites, and world-class leadership cannot be caught on a short cassette tape. This is especially true of spiritual things. The young man's problem is that he thinks he is better equipped than he actually is. Not knowing what he doesn't know, he continues to be ignorant of his ignorance. He wants to be treated as a world-class leader without world-class preparation. His world needs expanding. His drive should not be limited to local survival or even local success. His potential is much bigger than that, and, I might say, yours is too. But to see one's potential in its full range of possibilities is more terrifying than exciting. It is a powerful, overwhelming thing that drives one to a world of extremes. This young man should be deeply challenged by his elders to be a world-class, powerful leader. He definitely has the potential. Instead, he has been encouraged to be a little minion who has considerable vocational skills in the details of ministry, organization, and keeping his cautious elders happy. In fact, he and numerous others like him have been intentionally held away from such possibilities. This is a shame. This is a tragedy. This young man and many others like him remain seriously lacking in the arena of the great, the terrible, the mighty. Like many, he is a product of a generation of the instant and the safe. A vast range of rich, complex, and multi-layered possibilities lies beyond him because of his preoccupation with the minutiae of ministry. Of this larger world, he, along with numerous others, knows little or nothing, and will likely never know.

It is somewhat embarrassing to go to meetings and conferences and see these who know so much about the latest dress, fashions, jokes, and jargon. They know about the hottest sports teams and how to maintain a certain persona of being "in the know," when in reality they sorely lack substance, depth, and broad understanding. With little engagement in prayer and only rare occasions of in-depth study, they crassly continue to posture as those "in the know." Blessed with this world's goods in an abundance never before known, many could say to the beggar at the gate Beautiful, "Silver and gold have I, but what you need have I little or none." In an alarming number of cases, the degree of leisure, pleasure, and sophomoric shallowness found behind the posture of spiritual authority borders on the obscene. It is a masquerading of the shallows as being the deep, all of which leads to charismatic folly.

A sobering reality is that people are putting their eternal destiny in the hands of such leaders. The entire lives of those who follow these leaders will be profoundly influenced by the degree, or lack thereof, of wisdom and farsightedness of the leaders' decisions. Their success in the marketplaces of life will be affected. These decisions will affect marriages. Eternal destinies of parents and children hang in the balance. The downline repercussions of decisions of a spiritual leader can reverberate for generations. There is no other job, no other leadership position, no other profession in which a leader's decisions carry such weighty consequences and enduring ramifications. Spiritual leadership is tantamount to doing business in the deepest of the deep. When done by the unprepared, the casual, or those presumptuous and self-obsessed, the results are disastrous. To minister in the deep, one must voyage in the deep, live in the deep, be acquainted with the deep, understand guiding principles for navigating in the deep and respect the deep. To launch into the deep is to stretch one's possibilities to the extreme, to broaden and deepen every aspect of self that has to do with one's work, to carefully connect with righteous greatness wherever it is found, and to escape the bondage of the daily press of life. It is separation. It is deep praying and groanings which cannot be uttered. It is descending into places so deep and, in some cases, so dark as to leave one awestruck and often terrified at the yawning abyss before them. It is to stand at the portal of life and death and being. There is no other way. Someone must go. For where no ship is launched, it is futile to await a return loaded with treasure. All the prophecies in the world will never bring home that which never departed.

Preparing Ships and Sailors

Every individual is, in one sense, a captain of his own ship. He and his ship are one. Regardless of charts, equipment, preparation, and supplies, the ship is the essential thing. If the ship is not properly prepared, the sailors will not return. Wise captains are aware that the ship is the vessel upon which they are depending to take them to their goals. Thus, for leaders, the terms "preparation" and "ship" become almost synonymous. Preparation is the hull that is swabbed with the pitch of faith. Preparation is patient understanding of connectedness, of cuts and joints and tightly fitting boards, of pegs that firmly attach, and of careful and knowing application of glues and tars to prevent leaks. Ships are built in harbors but their seaworthiness is never really known until they are committed to the deep. So it is with leaders. Acquaintance with maintenance procedures, care of the sails, knowledge of supplies needed—all of this and more is required before one goes racing off to sea. Much of this is learned by helping on ships that belong to others. Those who refuse to learn by helping on the ships of others usually find themselves ill-prepared for later guiding their own.

Even passion cannot substitute for preparation. Some things are gained only by a patient process in formal, structured settings. This is especially important for our youth to realize. Once the appropriate time for preparation for spiritual leadership is passed without having been taken advantage of, that leadership is usually crippled from ever being what it could have been. Some, under the illusion that "passion is everything," later end up severely handicapped. Some ignore the necessity of developing even the most basic of ministry leadership skills, such as reading and writing. Knowing a lot about prayer but nothing about Paul is not healthy. How can one minister effectively and powerfully on an ongoing basis while possessing only a cursory knowledge of the Word? If doctors, lawyers, and engineers prepare long and hard, how much longer and harder should those called of God prepare? Can the importance of their work compare to this work? How deeply can one bring ongoing leadership to mankind while lacking, for example, a deep scriptural understanding of man? Passion alone cannot bring this. Efficiency in practical administration, business, finances, and organization cannot bring this. Management skills are not enough. Humans need spiritual food. No hunger for food is more real than the hunger of the soul for nutrition. Man shall not live by bread alone, but by every word that proceedeth out of the mouth of God. There is a spiritual bread. As surely as there is nutrition, there is spiritual nutrition. However, even this bread, regardless of how well prepared, like all other things in spiritual leadership, must be cast upon the waters.

To captain one's ship, all of the above are needed. But there is more. As important as these are, none are more important than knowledge of and respect for the deep itself and for sailing conditions. Knowledge of weather, wind, water, and ballast–the sailor must master them all.

A friend of mine, along with his wife and son, owned and lived on a large sailing vessel for several years. They sailed hundreds of miles up and down the coast of California and Mexico. At his invitation, my wife and I sailed with him and his wife one day. While in the galley eating, visiting and discussing the challenges of sailing, he explained to us that great seamen can be so attuned to the ship and to the sea that they can actually lie in their bunk in their cabin in the bottom of the ship and detect if the ship is off course by simply listening to the sound of the water as the boat moves through it. Sensitivity and experience make them wise to the way of the deep.

What a contrast to the jocular souls on deck who are jesting their way though life! Filled with foolishness and immaturity, these approach the holy and the noble with ignorance and disdain and trample sacred whispers from the mouths of angels beneath hob-nailed boots of callousness. Lacking appreciation of the honor to be bearers of the only saving, galactic message earth has ever received, they bray out their fetid breath like the untamed, unrefined that they are. Flee, young man, from the careless, the casual, the cynical!

In the days before aircraft, there were few classes of people who contributed more to national wealth and greatness than those who "went down to the sea in ships." The existence and prosperity of a nation depended upon the success of its sailors. In her days of power, England was passionate about her sailors. Like Spain, Portugal, and France before, her most popular songs were of the sea, and her most emotional stories of national victories were stories of sea battles. Many of her greatest heroes were her sailors.

Sailing was dangerous business. Those who remained behind on land often had little or no idea of the dangers involved in the process of going out and coming back. The general populace only knew that sailors went to mysterious, faraway lands and places. Nevertheless, the nations' sailors were held in the highest esteem. If nothing else was understood about them, there was an awareness by wise men that they were essential to prosperity and survival. Nations with poor sailors were invariably secondary. Nations with world power won it and held it in proportion to the boldness, prowess, and courage of their sailors. The church is no different. Love them or hate them, it is the sailors who are the core leaders.

As leaders, sailors led the way to discovery and prosperity. They were visionaries. Unable to see their goal or follow a rutted road, they had to understand the rhythms of the sea and the alignment of the heavens. Here again we are confronted with two concepts which are core to leadership: rhythm and alignment.

Sailors were lonely. The peculiar circumstances of a sailor's life withdrew him from many everyday influences. Absent for long periods from even his dearest relationships, casual acquaintances were almost non-existent. The world of the sailor was at once both severely confining and extremely liberating. The ship's boundaries were his boundaries, his world. It was a "micro" world. At the same time, he was dynamically integrated with the stars, the wind, the heavens–the "macro" world. He was away, sailing from vision to vision. He may not have ever returned. Some did not. But without the careful going and returning of a nation's sailors, poverty, isolation, and even starvation were continually lurking threats.

One cannot always tell who are sailors and who are not. Many wear the uniform, but are not sailors. Their followers are victimized by the charade. In the world of the spirit, it is no different. Everyone wants the sailors' glory, but few want the risks, the fears, the daunting and very real challenges. Those who go there, however, and experience "His wonders in the deep," are never the same. The sea marks them. Wonders experienced far from shore change them. They become different, set apart. More than a uniform is required to enter this exclusive group.

Chapter 3

The Primordial Deep

What is "the deep"? In many respects, this is a difficult question to answer. There is a need to talk about going to the deep and to discuss results of coming through the deep. Discussion should include examples of what leadership emerges from the deep. But what is the deep? Only the Bible can answer this question.

There is a path that leads to the edge of the deep. In one sense, this edge is never on the same level as the deep itself. The deep is far below. No one knows how far down it is or ultimately how deep it is.

Careful reading of the Bible reveals "the deep" to be an oft-recurring theme in scripture. The psalmist marvels, exclaiming: *"O Lord, how great are thy works! And thy thoughts are very deep"* (Psalm 92:5). He further observes, *"Deep calleth unto deep at the noise of thy waterspouts. All thy waves and thy billows are gone over me"* (Psalm 42:7). These scriptures, in the context of human spirituality, clearly imply that the "deep" of a human responds to the divine "deep," forging a profound human/divine relationship. So much of life is spent dabbling in the shallows. Sometimes the sludge of the trivial and the banal must be resolutely swept aside so as to rediscover the possibility of penetrating into the substance of this deep. God is deep. His divine deep calls to the deep of the individual, tapping into the deepest place in man.

- **The deep has a mysterious "call,"** a spiritual beckoning, a gentle but insistent urging. When combined with Christ's call to *"Launch out into the deep"* (Luke 5:4), we see it also as an urgent invitation and encouragement by Christ to push off into the deep. Most certainly the human heart hungers for the deep, but human rebellion resists it mightily.

- **The deep is hidden.** Genesis 49:25 speaks of *"blessings of the deep which lieth under...."* Surface living is once and for all abandoned. It is no wonder, then, that Christ directs us to *"Launch out into the deep"* (Luke 5:4). The disciples discovered that there are no great catches in the shallows.

- **The deep has "monsters" in it.** To add to the treachery of the deep, monsters live and lurk there. Leviathan is there (Job 41:1). The deep is so fearful that even demons are terrified of going there (Luke 8:31). No wonder there is such reticence to enter the deep! More than one has gone there, only to disappear beneath the surface and never return. It is strange and unfamiliar territory and is not a place for the novice, the casual, the cavalier.

The equating of the deep as the place of demons is common in Jewish literature as well as in scripture. In the gospels, gaining power over the sea is equated with gaining power over demonic forces (Mark 4:35-41; 6:45-50). Scripture positions the account of the stormy, screeching sea directly before the account of the shrill demonic insanity of the wild man of Gadara. Both the sea and the man are wildly out of control. There are shocking stories filled with descriptions of terror, astonishment, and begging. Nothing in human, medical or nautical skill is sufficient to tame or bind either. However, numerous scholars have correctly noted the remarkable fact that the language Jesus used to tame the sea is the language of exorcism common to Him in casting out demons. The unmistakable conclusion is that the demonic forces use the deep (i.e., the sea) to attempt to destroy both Jesus and the disciples but fail to do so. Jesus stymies their aggressive, destructive intent with His rebukes. Thus, the great stillness of wind and water resulting from Jesus' spoken command is very much the same as the calm of the delivered man sitting clothed and sane at the feet of Jesus. The enormous power of Jesus is punctuated by the fact that demonic use of the sea in 4:35-41 is clearly riveted on the intent of bringing about the watery destruction of both Jesus and the disciples in the deep. However, instead of succeeding in this intent, the reverse is true. Demonic forces are defeated on the sea. However, Jesus is not through with them. He confronts them again in the demoniac. This time, not only does He defeat them again, but He uses the very sea they intended to use to destroy Him, and sends them plunging into the sea in the swine to their destruction. He places an exclamation point on His absolute and complete domination of them and their attempts to destroy. Not only does He defeat them, He thoroughly smashes them, wrecking their house as well as their schemes. With unyielding determination, He drives them to utter banishment in the deep. Thus, the character of the sea miracles is seen, not only as power over natural forces, but as an extension of the confrontation of Jesus with the forces of evil. These encounters are not accidental. He intentionally confronts demonic strongholds and enters into the deepest citadels of hostile territory to do battle and to destroy these strongholds.

These accounts, along with numerous others, reveal the violent and unrelenting nature of Christ's determination. This is in dramatic contrast to His extreme tolerance and patience with humans. We can only conclude that His uncompromising dealings with the demonic stems from His knowledge of their unmitigated evil nature. They have no conscience. Their hatred, rebellion, and malevolent nature is totally bent on destruction. Dedicated to lawlessness, they are bankrupt of any redeemable qualities. Any leader who does not realize this is certain to be defeated. This is not a battle with people, but rather, with powerful, twisted, reprobate, raging, vicious spirits. To underestimate the concentrated, unadulterated nature of evil at this level is a mistake. It is beyond logic, beyond reasoning, beyond negotiation.

This uncompromising stance of Christ is in direct contrast to that which is around Him. The world in which He ministers has become accustomed to living with the demonic. This familiarity has developed into an accepted reality which they have come to accept as normal. This is done to the extent that any alternative is viewed as unacceptable, as an intrusion on their way of life, or as something to be resisted. A completely convoluted line of reasoning is developed in which liberty and freedom are viewed as terrifying. The inhabitants of Gadera are willing to live with less than the optimum. The demons also seek a negotiated settlement. But Christ will have none of it. He has come to unsettle this long-established order of demonism. While appearing to grant the demons' request to enter the swine, He is, in reality, simply using the swine as a vehicle to transport the entire feral community of demons to their banishment.

How can such overwhelming powers be defeated? Who is equal to such a challenge? Observing the way Jesus handles these challenges reveals the tremendous triumphant power which is the outgrowth of the primary spiritual event instant which provided the substructure for His ministry.

The deep of the earth is old, as is the earth itself. Who knows fully what has been or what is here now? For example, on islands near the earth's frozen pole, thousands of monkey bones have been discovered. How did the monkeys, who require temperate zones to survive, get there? No one knows. Roman historians Suetonius and Josephus both record that in Palestine in the days of Christ, human bones of giant size were displayed in museums. Where did they come from? The explanations for these phenomena are shrouded in mystery. Other strange archaeological discoveries reveal fossilized remains of creatures with estimated lengths of 120 feet and crocodiles 40 feet long, weighing 20 times as much as crocodiles weigh today! These archeological finds are changing the way we see our world and increasing its mystery. In the same sense, the Bible reveals the spirit world to be equally real and mysterious. While some may doubt it, these realities are questionable only to those who have not walked in the world of the spirit. Some will scoff, others will attempt to explain all away as imaginary, and still others will try to manufacture a rational explanation. However, scripture addresses realities for which the reductionist language of higher education, psychology, sociology, and such cannot account. That there are malevolent and shadowy forces that oppose humanity is a reality repeatedly validated. Or, as Yancey (2001) states, no force in nature can explain these things, but they are obviously of a "malevolent force from supernature."

"For we wrestle not against flesh and blood, but against principalities, against powers, against the rulers of the darkness of this world, against spiritual wickedness in high places."   Ephesians 6:12

How else can one explain the utter viciousness that exists in the world? Nevertheless, there are many scriptures that resolutely and unquestionably attest to the power of the believer and the church over all aspects of these creatures of the dark.

"Thou breakest the heads of leviathan in pieces, and gavest him to be meat to the people inhabiting the wilderness."   Psalm 74:14

"The sea is dangerous and its storms terrible, but the obstacles have never been sufficient reason to remain

ashore...unlike the mediocre, intrepid spirits seek victory over these things that seem impossible...it is with an iron will that they embark on the most daring of all endeavors...to meet the shadowy future without fear and conquer the unknown."

- Ferdinand Magellan

- **The deep, though treacherous, has protection.** *"In his hand are the deep places..."* (Psalm 95:4). When the surface and seeming safety is far away, it is faith in His promises that sustain. Thus, Peter calls them "precious promises."
- **The deep is the secret place of great success.** Even though the deep is treacherous, there is assurance to the traveler doing business in the deep: *"They that go down...in ships...he bringeth them unto their desired haven"* (Psalm 107:23, 30). So what is "the deep" and the "great waters" from which we seek to return with spiritual prosperity and success? From where did the idea of the deep originate?

Origins of the Deep

"The deep" is a concept that is far more ancient than man. The deep is older than life on earth as we know it. The deep itself comes from deep within the primal beginning of reality. Older than mountains, older than sunrise and sunset, it is connected closely with ancient judgment and chaos. First mention of the deep is in the first chapter of the first book of the Bible (as it should be).

"And the earth was without form and void; and darkness was upon the face of the deep. And the Spirit of God moved upon the face of the waters."

Genesis 1:2

Here the earth story begins with "great waters" and "the deep." How deep was the deep? No one knows. The deep is a seminal subject of scripture. Water is depicted as a deep and mysterious subterranean world. It is a foreboding place, but it is also the place from which land and life emerge and upon which the earth continually depends. Water, or the deep, becomes a metaphor for both chaos and potential. The Bible scarcely opens before this usage appears. The deep is chaos and is "unmoved" in the sense that it is undeveloped potential. It could conceivably remain deep, foreboding, and chaotic forever. It is in an intermediate state between nothing and something. Having no form, it is, nevertheless, something. It contains potential, but only latently. The possibilities are deep (no one knows how deep) but shapeless. It is potential without formation. From the secret of the deep emerges that which is unobserved by casual viewing.

Potential is submerged in the deep of possibility, yet without form. In this deep lies the answer to the gap between potential and fulfillment. Until it takes concrete form, potential is void, empty, and meaningless. Totally unstructured and in an uncentered state of being, it lacks core or mass. Without a catalyst, the water remains as such and darkness continues on the face of the deep. Darkness shrouds the deep, hiding its potential. Light is needed to cause the darkness to flee.

How long did such potential lie silently unbothered, brooded over but never actualized? One year? A thousand years? Millions of years? We do not know. Like the earth itself, it is equally possible for the deep of an individual to lie forever unmoved. It does not move from potential to formation in and of itself. A creative action is required to trigger the necessary movement for form to rise from non-form. How does this happen?

Two catalysts, both found in Genesis chapter one, appear to work in tandem to activate formation from out of the deep. One is the moving of the Spirit. The other is the spoken divine Creative Word.

Activation of Formation

How long was the earth inundated under the void and deep of Genesis 1:2? Until recently, scientists believed that the earth was about four billion years old, with life appearing only in the last six hundred million years. Now many scientists claim that geologic evidence is revealing a very different picture. They believe life originated almost instantaneously with the emergence of the earth. Other scientists, however, scoff at such concepts. Obviously, no one knows how long the earth was inundated in chaos. However, scripturally, we can determine that that which was in chaos was abandoned by God to destructive forces and was under judgment. No solution remained other than divine action. This action was required to ignite the change process. Thus, the writer of Genesis declares, *"And the Spirit of God moved upon the face of the waters"* (1:2).

The Moving of the Spirit

The moving of the Spirit is the initial action that causes potential to become concrete reality. Without the moving of the Spirit, nothing happens. This is inalterable.

What initially causes the Spirit to move? Genesis does not tell us. What causes the Spirit to call one out of the world or to call one to ministry? Why does one feel a call this way and another that way? These are mysteries hidden in the wisdom of God (John 3:8). This initial "call" of God, or the move of the Spirit upon the face of the deep of individual potential, is a sovereign act. God owns so God chooses. This is not a tentative, apologetic call. God fully expects one to follow the call. The believer is God's property and is in no position to bargain. God is going to make something and chooses to use this material or that. If the called one dies in the process of fulfilling his/her call, then so be it, for God is more concerned with His mission than the length of the minister's life on earth. The calling is without repentance.

As God's anointed, no prophet is greater than John the Baptist. His entire life is preparation for a ministry of only a few days. His call places him at odds with the authorities. He never escapes this pressure. His life is cut short, he experiences little or no recorded leisure, and he dies a premature and ignominious death that appears altogether to be defeat at the hands of a rebuked but defiant, wicked woman. No one comes to his aid. No one advocates for his innocence. His bloody, severed head is brought in to be gloated over and held in derision. His precious, valuable life is brutally cut short by vicious, drunken adulterers. Does God intervene? No. To God, it doesn't matter. God has a purpose that transcends John's physical welfare. The sooner this fact is understood and accepted–totally and without reservation–the sooner true spiritual formation begins. This submission, this unquestioning, complete, unreserved, willing, total surrender of self is central to the formative process. It is easier said than done. Nevertheless, when the Spirit moves on that which has the potential for form, whether the subject is the earth or a human, God inexorably moves toward the fulfilling of His purposes. Spiritual formation and vision are subjects that have received little, if any, attention from writers of religious books. A few years ago, I conducted a search for religious literature on the subject of "vision," a subject which, as we shall later see, is inextricably linked to leadership. Such literature is extremely scarce. Hardly a volume can be found that significantly addresses this vital subject. It is easier to find secular books that address the subject of "vision," but these are written primarily for business people and entrepreneurial types. These books can be helpful, but they are limited in scope. Lacking the penetrating depth of theology, they only go so far. Like leading cattle, they move their readers to where there is some "pasture," but it is limited. When pursuing the answer to effective leadership, one is eventually confronted with the need to understand spiritual matters. However, when writers of secular books arrive at this juncture, most of them stop. The "moving of the Spirit upon the face of the deep" is a gate that they choose to leave unopened, possibly because of marketing reasons, or possibly because of fear of the unknown. This is the gate that stands precisely between secularism and spirituality. The secular is caught in an awareness that the core of leadership is found in the spiritual, but is hesitant to go there. Therefore, the problem remains that leadership studies bog down when they attempt to stand alone and apart from the theological and spiritual. Disconnecting leadership studies from spiritual formation and vision bifurcates the subject. True greatness in leadership derives only from this very plunge into spiritual formation.

Current writers on the subject of leadership and vision are almost exclusively educators, motivators, and business people. Even those who write from a religious viewpoint often intentionally water down the spiritual aspects. This is not a criticism, for any discussion of the subject is perhaps better than none. In fact, as little as 40 years ago, if someone would have suggested, "We need vision to make this business successful," they very well may have been perceived as a little strange and esoteric. In contrast, even a cursory reading of the Bible shows spiritual formation and vision to be at the very core of great leadership and true greatness. Since secular writers are not theologians and often have an aversion to overt references to the Bible, they miss this core in their search for answers. Therefore, treatment of such subjects often comes to the gate of spirituality and stops. Here the herd mills, partly satisfied to have come this far, but intuitively aware that there is more. Desirous to feed in the tall, verdant pasture just across the fence, they seek to go beyond the locked gate. Only the true apostolic shepherd can lead them there. This gives the authentic apostolic leader a clear advantage in depth and breadth of leadership. This advantage is not a myth, not a motivational ploy. It is a fact—a fact that all righteous spiritual leaders need to grasp boldly and confidently and exploit to the fullest. Only "spirituals" can go through the aforementioned "locked gate." This book has to do with unlocking and passing through that gate.

It is not yet certain whether the gate should be unlocked for everyone. There is, indeed, wonderful "pasture" there. However, the area contains large, unexplored spiritual areas with precipitous cliffs and drop-offs into the very deep sea whose breadth and depth remain unplumbed. Those who are not sobered by such knowledge should perhaps stay on the supposed "safe" side of the gate.

In years gone by, the thought of teaching leadership as a subject in universities was often opposed. Educators feared that "unworthies" would learn techniques and use them to manipulate people. Some have cited Hitler and Stalin as examples of why leadership studies perhaps should not be taught. Further, people interested in such things may not only become a danger to others, but may plunge unaware into areas of personal danger. They may take long, hard falls from which they never return. Where is the bottom? Who knows? Downward they fall, faster and faster, hurtling through space with no orbit, deeper and deeper into the inky abyss. To use the language of Christ's brother, they become *"....wandering stars, to whom is reserved the blackness of darkness forever"* (Jude 1:13).

On the other hand, a deep level of commitment is the only avenue to spiritual power. One cannot do great things for God without "taking the voyage" into the world of the spirit. It is powerful company, *"...seeing we also are compassed about with so great a cloud of witnesses...,"* the writer of Hebrews exclaims. We are *"...standing before the angel of the Lord, and Satan standing at his right hand to resist him"* (Zechariah 3:1). Great potential, great danger, great stakes! They always go together. In this vein, God extends a stunning promise:

> *"If thou wilt walk in my ways, and if thou wilt keep my charge, then thou shalt also judge my house, and shalt also keep my courts, and I will give thee places to walk among these that stand by."*   Zechariah 3:7

Here is true power for mission. Here is real authority. Here is enablement. Here is the place of success and failure, a road strewn with the petals of victors as well as the carcasses of failures. Upon reaching the "tipping point," one is inevitably plunged into these previously unexplored areas—high places, deep places, uncertain places, murky places. And lonely places. Much like a sailor and the sea.

In observing biblical models, one cannot help but see that there is virtually no example of great leadership that was not preceded by extensive training. The concept that "God anoints and, bless God, that's enough for me" is, if it is true, effective on one level. Episodic and isolated examples can be found in which God uses someone mightily who lacks training. This is good and true. However, in the development of great leadership, this is not the norm, and it is not the case where leaders are being chosen for the "long haul." Moses, Joshua, David, Elisha, and Christ's disciples all exemplify this truth regarding training. Every church should provide opportunity for exposure to such training.

There is a necessary training process. How many times has this been witnessed in church work? The preacher is a great evangelist–powerful, effective, impacting. We see him this way. He sees himself this way. He is, indeed, truly so, at least as an evangelist. But then he assumes the pastorate of a church. The sermons run out. Decisions must be made. Families must be nurtured. Young people must be led. Vision and direction must be given. Trainees must be mentored. Administrative issues must be dealt with. Strongholds must now be breached, entered, and conquered. And, perhaps most demanding of all, people must be fed spiritual meat—for days, for months, for years, possibly for decades. The resilience of saints who have survived year after year on gruel and the thinnest of soups is amazing!

Affective development (i.e., sensitivity, feelings, awareness) is equally critical to spiritual leadership training. There is no substitute for a red-hot apostolic atmosphere exuding the power of God, deliverance, victory, and joy. Here, learning is caught rather than taught. One cannot develop this aspect of training in solitude. It is developed in the midst of the worshiping body, in the swirl and repeated visitation of the positive, the robust, the glorious, the mysterious, and the other-worldly. Full preparation for leadership on any level is not possible apart from this exposure to the presence of God in a worshiping church. Cognitive learning divorced from this affective component spells certain death to greatness in leadership and often produces a brand of parched intellectualism bereft of spiritual life and richness. Proof of this is the educated sterility which permeates large portions of today's academia and business communities, as well as the mainline denominational church world.

A prerequisite to profound spiritual formation is formation of the spiritual, inner self. This includes deep, cathartic, personal, spiritual experiences found only in extended and deep sessions of personal prayer and communication with God. This is a major element of the foundation upon which all else is built. Without this wonder-full, entrancing, transforming time spent alone (even if in a crowd) with

God, there is no spiritual greatness. It is the moving of the Spirit upon the personal soul that is necessary for form to rise out of mere potential.

The Creative Word

The first event in spiritual formation recorded in Genesis chapter one is the moving of the Spirit upon the face of the deep. The second event that brings spiritual formation is God's Word. The Spirit moves, then comes the Creative Word. *"And God said..."* (Genesis 1:3). Divine utterance is a prerequisite to formation. Regardless of how much the Spirit moves, it is the Word that brings form out of chaos.

Nothing "is" that has not resulted from the utterance of the Creative Word. *"And God said let there be..."* is the creative formula for all that exists—plants, animals, dirt, rocks, elements, planets, every heavenly body, humans, angels, Heaven, earth, and all else. There is no reality of any kind apart from that which is spoken into existence by the Word of God. There is no other creative source or process existent other than this Word.

> *"In the beginning was the Word...All things were made by him; and without him was not any thing made that was made."* John 1:1,3

"All things" is inclusive of anything that has "being," whether physical or spiritual, visible or invisible. There is no other reality, material or immaterial, than that which is spoken into being by the divine Creative Word.

This tandem manifestation of the Spirit and the Word is a recurring pattern throughout scripture. Downplaying the role of the one in an attempt to accentuate the other is a mistake. Both are essential elements of divine creative actions. The "moving of the Spirit" indicates that God is in action. Wherever this happens, there is an observable result. Abraham first experiences the "smoking furnace" and "burning lamp"—both being actions of God. Then Abraham receives verbal affirmation of God's covenant by the Word of God. With this covenant, God promises that He will form a people out of Abraham's descendants. At Sinai, the people experience a manifestation of God in action on the mountain. Following this is the giving of the Word written on tablets of stone. Out of this Creative Word, a people is formed. They can now develop identity, common language, law, culture, goals, purpose, aspirations, etc. An additional example that reveals this Spirit and Word pattern is the baptism of Jesus. As Christ arises out of the chaotic swirl of the waters of baptism (cp. Genesis 1:2), praying (Luke 3:21), all three synoptics record the Spirit descending followed by the voice of God speaking. Here again is formation. A Messiah is being formed.

Perhaps the greatest creative act of spiritual formation is the birth of the church on the day of Pentecost. Here, as in Genesis chapter one, the Spirit first moves. *"And suddenly there came a sound from heaven as of a rushing mighty wind (Gr., "pneuma," wind, breath, spirit), and it filled all the house where they were sitting"* (Acts 2:2). Following this moving of the "wind" (breath, Spirit), miraculous spiritual formation and creation takes place in each of the 120 as God speaks through them with other tongues. The "voice from heaven" (i.e., Word of God) at Christ's baptism is now manifested in the wind that has come to them "from heaven." This Spirit-Wind moves into the believers, and God, who previously creatively spoke from Heaven (at both Sinai and also at Christ's baptism), now speaks from within these newly-filled with His Spirit. The Creative Word is uttered from them and through them. Henceforth, this same Creative Word now speaks through the believer to *"ask what ye will, and it shall be done."* Thus, spiritual formation of a people with a heavenly identity is an ongoing phenomenon. *"Therefore, if any man be in Christ, he is a new creature..."* (2 Corinthians 5:17).

In these last days, anointed preaching and proclamation is the medium through which the Creative Word enters the affairs of men and continues His creative work of forming a new people. The Spirit and Word of Genesis 1:2 is the same that Israel experienced at Sinai and that Christ experienced at His baptism. It now indwells believers. The Spirit-filled believers become the source of divine creative activity as the Spirit moves through them issuing forth with prophetic utterance.

Where there is no divine Word, there is an absence of form. The spoken Creative Word is the source of all things. Hence, where the Creative Word has not spoken, there is either nothing or only shifting, unstructured chaos. All is liquid and uncertain. Unpredictability and formlessness is the only reality. It is a state of utter rootlessness too terrifying to ponder. Even demons experience horror at the possibility of returning into this formless state (Luke 8:31).

Why is it so terrifying and horrifying? We are aware that we can lose our human "being." This fear of loss of being, of "non-being," is something beyond us, yet something to which we sense we could be subjected. It is worse than the fear of death. To not "be" is the ultimate fear.

So what sustains that which has being? Science has no answer for this, but theology does. Scripture is clear that the thing that sustains all that has being is the Word of God (Colossians 1:17).

In contrast to the Word as the ultimate and sole source of all that is, Satan's approach to Eve is based on the idea that there is an alternate world. Satan argues that God is trying to prevent Adam and Eve from becoming God-like. He reasons that God doesn't want them to experience this other reality and is, therefore, stifling their potential. The convoluted implication is that God is violating their freedom and suppressing their development and formation. Of course, this is all a lie. Apart from the Creative Word, there is no other reality, only illusion, deception, and delusion,

"For by him were all things created, that are in heaven, and that are in earth, visible and invisible, whether they be thrones, or dominions, or principalities, or powers: all things were created by him, and for him..."

Colossians 1:16

Use of logic against God's Word is forbidden. Ray Anderson (1978) explains that the Creative Word is self-authenticating–it neither needs nor accepts outside validation. In fact, implicit in the Word is a judgment against all questions that could be raised in hopes of verifying the Word on some basis independent of the Word itself. Not only does the Word not need validation outside of itself, it judges all such attempts.

In this light, Anderson points out that Abraham and Sarah obviously think they are "helping" God by devising a way to bring about the birth of a son. Has not God promised a son, and are not the physical possibilities of that taking place by Sarah too remote to consider? Are they not to use the faculties that God has given them to think, to plan, and to bring about the birth of the promised son? Shouldn't one use logic? Thus Abraham devises a way to bring his heir into the world. He supposes he has saved the day by his ingenuity. This appears to him to be true for a long time, years in fact. However, eventually the Word comes again that Sarah will have a baby. This is incredible to them, and, to Abraham, it seems unnecessary. For 13 years, Abraham has taught Ishmael that he is the heir who can fulfill God's Word. He is his boy. For Abraham, the coming of the promised son of the Creative Word is a very traumatic and difficult time. He has pinned his hopes on Ishmael. When word comes again from God that Isaac is to be born, Abraham, in a possible final, frantic hope to make Ishmael the child of promise, circumcises both himself and Ishmael, as well as his entire male household. *"O that Ishmael might live before thee!"* he pleads (Genesis17:18). But the answer is, "No." The Creative

Word has indeed spoken a promised son, but Ishmael is not it. In this context, from God's view, Abraham has never had, nor does he yet have, the promised son. God says, "Sarah, your wife, shall bear you a son." In the refining fires of final judgment, how many human efforts will never receive recognition that they existed? Can anything be genuine, good, or beautiful if it is independent of the divine Word? To favor the contrivings of the human mind over the divine Word is to clutch illusion. Outside of the Creative Word, nothing is. In contrast to Adam and Eve, Abraham finally acquiesces and obeys the divine Word. However, it drastically upsets his entire house. All that Ishmael has been taught has to be untaught. God responds, *"...as for Ishmael I have heard thee...But my covenant I will establish with Isaac. And He left off talking with him..."* (Genesis 17:20, 21, 22). And he left off talking with him. What an astonishing statement! God quits talking. He simply has nothing else to say on the subject. There is nothing left to say beyond the divine spoken Word.

Entrance of Light

Genesis chapter one reveals the process by which formation takes place. From formless, empty shapelessness, the process of formation begins with the moving of the Spirit of God and continues with utterance from the Creative Word. The third event in formation is the creation of light. *"And God said, let there be light, and there was light"* (Genesis 1:3).

Where the Spirit moves and the Creative Word is spoken, light comes. Light enables one to see. Vision depends on light. Revelation depends on light. *"The eyes of your understanding being enlightened that ye may know..."* (Ephesians 1:18). In genuine ministry, one "sees before one does" (cp. John 5:19).

Life is dependent upon light. Where there is no light, there is no life. The entire process of photosynthesis is light-dependent. From both the Old Testament tabernacle as well as Apostle Paul, we see a contrast between what can be seen by natural light as opposed to what can be seen by spiritual "light." The Old Testament tabernacle was specifically designed so interior ministry was done without natural light. The ministry had only the light from the candlesticks. In the New Testament, Paul draws a clear distinction between the natural mind and the things of the Spirit (1 Corinthians 2). He plainly states that the natural man receiveth not the things of the Spirit. To the Ephesians, he further declares:

> *"The eyes of your understanding being enlightened; that ye may know what is the hope of his calling, and what the riches of the glory of his inheritance in the saints..."*   *Ephesians 1:18*

Formation Emerges

All of the above—the Spirit moving, the Creative Word speaking, and the entrance of light—are precedents to actual formation. In our discussion of the formation of the physical earth, we have yet to see emergence of land (i.e., form) out of water. We have yet to see the emergence of potential into concrete, realized form. Just as this physical formation is a product of the Spirit, the Word and light, so is spiritual formation. It is a core truth regarding effective ministry. It is no accident that the first three verses of the Bible contain all three. Herein lie the constituent agents of spiritual formation.

Form finally emerges in verse nine. Here dry land appears. As opposed to nothingness, it is "real" estate.

Formation emerges from possibility. The deep is uncentered and unformed. But with the emergence of form comes definition. It is stable and has specificity and identity, and it is able to bear the weight of further formation that will eventually arise from, and be built upon, this initial formation. Potential, by itself, has no "place." But now, formation has "whereness" and sufficient density for habitation and further creativity. From far under the surface, potential has emerged and burst forth into form. What was once only dynamic possibility is now formed into reality.

Likewise, spiritual formation arises from the deep of the individual. It is only out of the "deep" of one's being that one's potential can be realized. Most never know their potential because they shy away from these depths. In contrast, the Spirit draws us to "launch out into the deep"—the deep of our own God-formed possibilities. Here reside the "great waters" of human makeup. Here and here alone in one's life are found the works of the Lord and His wonders. Here is the place of deep and broad personal development through prayer, through reflection, through "coming aside," and through encounter with God. Perhaps until now you, the reader, have stood upon what others before you have formed. Others journeyed in the Spirit into dark recesses of their own deep to bring formation. Perhaps to this point, all formation with you, the reader, has been derived. But now, the call to "Launch out!" resonates in you. There is discontent with the shapeless irresponsibility of the shallows. The call to the sea can no longer be resisted. No person of depth escapes the spiritual aching and yearning for the distant rhythm of the sea and the entrancing alignment of the heavens. For this, there is absolutely no substitute.

A close reading of Psalm 107 reveals the exact description of the voyage. The writer describes waves *"...mounting to Heaven."* On top of a wave! And, oh, what a wave! The exhilaration of discovery, of success, of blessedness, of fulfilled purpose– indescribable joy! Glorious and victorious! There is nothing like it. But wait! Also, *"They go down again into the depths."* From intoxicating peaks and giddy heights, the sailor plunges out of sight into the depths of a dark, liquid canyon. Observing this process, the psalmist says, *"Their soul is melted because of trouble."* Whose soul? The soul of one who would *"...see the works of the Lord"* and *"His wonders in the deep."* There is no escaping these difficulties. Broken lines, tormenting winds, crumpled masts, ripped sails, insubordinate mates, rancid food—all are part of the journey. Discouragement, the jeering of a thousand laughing demons, public humiliation, and temporary failure all conspire to defeat such spiritual voyagers until finally, *"They reel to and fro and stagger like a drunken man!"* This is the lot of the voyager. Pride lost and skills exhausted, the leader sometimes continues to slog forward with nothing but mindless determination and commitment to the established goal. One's pride is repeatedly leveled until pliability emerges that the Potter can use to "form" what He desires without so much as a whimper of protest. It often seems the sea will destroy such a voyager before formation emerges. Sometimes it does. But there is hope. It can be done. When planning and maneuvering fail, *"Then they cry unto the Lord in their trouble, and He bringeth them out of their distresses. He maketh the storm a calm...Then are they glad...so he bringeth them unto their desired haven"* (Psalm 107:28-30). There is solace. People do make it. Voyagers do reach their God-given dreams and inspirations. People really do accomplish victories with universal impact. Great things do happen. There is a real greatness and it does reside in the potential of every believer. Others have gone there. You can too.

Emergence of Form upon Form

Genesis chapter one reveals a pattern of formation. With the initial formation of dry land, more formation rapidly begins to take place. Rather than a one-time event, a cycle of formation is set up. This cycle spirals wildly into the superabundant creation of life and fruitfulness. From the land that has emerged from the deep comes new forms of life: grass, herbs, trees and vines (Genesis 1: 11, 12). The earth has now gone from the nothingness of unformed potential to potentiality actualized. From this, it moves to production or fruitfulness—and such fruit! It spirals out a thousand ways in exponential life. Again, just as physical formation produces fruit, so likewise spiritual formation produces spiritual fruitfulness. Thus, the desired end of spiritual formation is not to simply admire the creation of form, but rather to produce fruit, and then to replenish and produce again and again. This is a never-ending, expanding cycle of new forms of beauty, glory, and abundance. Such becomes the life of an authentically spiritually-formed person. The tree is ultimately known by its fruit. A cycle of ongoing, fruit-producing formation takes place.

Where there is authentic formation, the potential for production is staggering. For years, scientists, Darwinists, and those over-using the "endangered species" label have issued dire predictions of the cessation of life on earth as we know it. They lament that man's so-called progress is destroying a large portion of earth's life. The truth is just the opposite! There are more life-forms on the face of the earth today than ever before. Life is creating an infinite number of possibilities (Wheatley and Kellner-Rogers, 1996). The process of creative formation out of chaos is clearly revealed in scripture, and the process of form emerging from potential and more form emerging from existing form repeats exponentially.

What percentage of one's potential can be expected to be realized? The answer is, no one knows. One's potential is so far beyond the imagination to conceive that no one has ever gone there. Is individual potential ever exhausted? The answer is a resounding "No!" There are no known limits or boundaries. The possibilities are virtually endless.

However, it is possible for one's actualized potential (i.e., potential that has become concrete reality) to slip away and return again to the deep. Those who allow such come under judgment. A "macrocosmic" example of this in the physical world is the flood of Noah's day. In the flood, the same earth at which we have been looking in Genesis chapter one had its form submerged once again beneath the deep. Formation was destroyed. Tragically, everything formed upon the initial formation of land was lost. It was cataclysmic. It was utterly disastrous. Life was destroyed. Form was destroyed. Only that which was aligned (through obedience) with the Creative Word survived. Everything outside of that Word was once more submerged into the chaos of the deep. Even then, however, potential remained intact and form eventually emerged once more from the depths. Upon re-emergence, God gave a promise that there would never cease to be seedtime and harvest. In other words, from now on, upon the face of the earth, there will always be physical form upon which other formation (i.e., plant, animal, and human life) takes place. If potential itself had been lost, it would not have been a flood, but rather, final destruction and decay into nothingness.

The book of Revelation predicts a time when there will be "no more sea." Earth will evidently have reached its fully formed state. This does not mean there will be no more potential for the earth to produce, but rather, earth formation will have become so permanent and so complete that the earth will have optimized its power to bring other forms (i.e., plant, animal, and human life) to reality. Based upon the land that has been formed, the process of going from potential to actualization to fruit-bearing will continue forever at an optimal level, spinning out what it produces into the universe.

This is also the ideal goal of one's leadership development—to be fully formed, fully optimized, and fully producing in regular cycles. It is a leadership that is ever replicating outward into one's universe. Herein lies one's purpose and mission. It is apparent that leading others begins in the interior rather than the exterior. It is not first about seeing others changed. Rather, it begins in seeing self changed. Self-formation precedes fruit bearing. The seedbed for great leadership lies deep within the interior recesses of the human heart and spirit. Spiritual formation for world-class leadership does not just "happen" to everyone who has experienced salvation. The potential is there, however, biblical models reveal that such formation is invariably accompanied by crisis. The crisis may be overtly induced by God or it may be brought about through events in one's life. From whatever the source, these events push one to an edge, a precipice. In some cases, it seems that some people are actually pushed by the Spirit over the edge. However, to go off this edge without a good deal of obedience, zeal, and passion having already been worked in an individual is to throw one into tremendous conflict and inner turmoil.

Someone has asked, "What is the defining moment, or, the edge, for me?" The answer is, "No one knows what the defining moment, or edge is for you, but if you ever reach it, you will know you have done so." God will know you are there and the enemy will know you are there. For Jonah, the defining moment was the call to Nineveh. For Israel, it was the Red Sea, and later, Jordan. For Jesus, it was His baptism. When Jesus set out from home one day to be baptized by John, did He know it would be a day that contained such extreme change? Did He, as a man, know what was about to crash in on Him when He arose from the water of baptism? From the evidence available, it seems doubtful that He was aware of the extent of the radical implications.

Are some people "fated" from birth for the deep? It is not certain, although it seems so. While every man has the power of choice, it is nevertheless true that John the Baptist, filled with the Holy Ghost from his mother's womb, was certainly marked, as was Jesus, Jeremiah, and others. While they evidently could have resisted the call, their purpose on earth preceded their birth. Some, however, seem to have attained these levels of leadership by other means. Moses was put in the deep by his mother. Samuel also "got there" seemingly because of his mother, at least at first. In contrast, the individual calls of David, Jonathan, and others seem to have been influenced by, and to contain, considerable elements of youthful zeal and radical commitment. In further contrast, Zacharias, the father of John the Baptist, plunged off over his head unexpectedly as an elderly man. In every case, this event was accompanied by upheaval and change so radical that their lives were never the same again.

What is the defining moment for you? For one thing, it is the point at which you lose your free will. It is the place where you leap, by faith, from the precipice of the safe, the familiar, and the comfortable into abandonment of self. It is the momentous step that sets you apart from the comfortable, the known, the rationally secure. It is the place where a specific vision for the Kingdom impacts you so compellingly as to sweep away all else before you and you are eaten up with the zeal of God's house. It is where God's will consumes and draws you in so completely that all else pales into insignificance. The edge is having the fruit that God wants produced in your life revealed to you, then submitting to–leaping into–the deep process, which produces the form, which ultimately produces the fruit. For spiritual ministry, the defining moment is stepping off into many hours of prayer and fasting and the Word–wrestling one's way to spiritual formation. The edge is where one hears from God and then sees, with clear definition, one's full ministry potential and calling.

Many men, even those mildly successful by outward standards, may have never been to this edge. In fact, they may have avoided it and been encouraged by controlling voices to stay away from it. Nevertheless, the biblical pattern is unmistakably clear. Where there is no leap, there is no greatness. Can this call, which would lead "over the edge," simply be ignored?

Going into and coming out of the deep challenges and alters the view of oneself and moves one from fuzziness to clarity. It gives unmistakable authority with God and man. It gives genuine authority in leadership and the spirit-world and, for a preacher, obvious authority in the pulpit. It makes one "another person." It gives insight into, and authority in, the multi-layered and sophisticated warfare of the subterranean forces that dictate world events. It makes one aware that the history of the visible is being determined largely by a history transpiring beneath the surface of the visible. Every human faculty is submitted to God. Ideally, every faculty is like soil producing new form from and out of itself.

All plant life, aquatic life, and animal-human life initially resided in the deep as mere potential. This was not remotely detectable on the surface. Neither could it be seen from analysis of the waters. Nevertheless, even though unactualized, it did, in fact, exist. Only God knows. One cannot estimate the degree of potential in any individual by observing the surface. This is true of creation as well as an individual whom God would anoint with great leadership. Potential is often well hidden. For example, Gideon is hiding, working to survive in fear and intimidation, when the angel appears with the greeting, "Gideon, thou mighty man of valor." Was the angel lying or using psychology? No. The fact is, God knew more about Gideon's potential than did Gideon himself. Potential cannot be analyzed and quantified. The human soil out of which greatness forms is often astonishing to observers. A root can arise out of dry ground.

Life, then, is the capacity for that which has "being" only as potential to take on concrete "being" in time and space. Once the process of Genesis 1:11 begins, life generates with wildly increasing volume and exploding variety. The movement of purpose in life is depicted in figure 7:

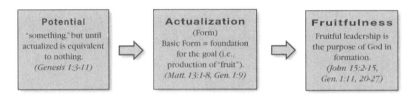

Figure 7

Chapter 4

Spiritual Form-ation

The sea-voyage of Psalm 107 points us toward the development of a biblical understanding of spiritual formation. This process of formation roughly parallels the formation of the earth. Scripture makes a point of emphasizing that man himself is drawn from the earth and is of the earth. Just as the Spirit moves (blows, breathes) upon the face of the deep, God "breathes" into man and he becomes a living soul. The spiritual parallel to this is found in the new birth; God's wind–or Spirit or breath–"blows" into the upper room as recorded in Acts 2, then blows or "breathes" into each believer. The Creative Word speaks through them (in other tongues). Enlightenment results. Once "dead in trespasses and sins" (Ephesians 2:1), life now erupts out of death. Spiritual form takes place as Christ is "formed" within. Fishermen and tax collectors blossom into world-class leaders. Christ, however, does not simply "blow" into man's body or mind, but rather, blows into the "deep" of man (i.e., his spirit). This is so powerful that out of his "innermost being" (John 7:38) is released a river of life and a breathtaking array of life-giving "charismata," or gifts. God now actually speaks creatively through the newly formed believer (1 Corinthians 12:10; 14:2).

Further, this "new creation man" (2 Corinthians 5:17), through this newly acquired divine sonship, is made capable of going beyond the previous limits of his own finitude and into the infinite (e.g., 1 Corinthians 12:8, 10). This is a staggering thought. Even a cursory glance at the ministries of Jesus and the apostles quickly validates the fact that apostolic power repeatedly enables believers to transcend finitudinal boundaries of time, space, and substance. Healings speed up nature's healing process supernaturally. Miracles restore life. A minister is transported supernaturally from one place to another. Remote events are inexplicably known about. The resurrected Christ exits a room with the doors and/or windows all closed–and does so after eating! Prison gates open of their own accord, addresses of places are revealed supernaturally, and visitors from another realm (i.e., angels) appear. In a world in which every man dies, the hope of salvation is called "life eternal" and is confidently preached without even a pause. Believers are given supernatural "gifts," which give them knowledge, power, utterance, wisdom and understanding, all of which transcend in various ways the constraints of time, space, and substance. *"Nothing shall be impossible unto you,"* declares Christ to His followers. They are expected not to balk at overwhelming odds, impossible tasks, and daunting opposition. Instead, they are cheerily encouraged to have faith that all is well, victory is assured, and that, *"I am with you."* Christ calmly bases this victory over the whole world, yea, the whole cosmos on His own victory by declaring, *"I have overcome the world."* Scripture unapologetically asserts His complete dominion over not only earth, but the entire universe. Indeed, He is clearly portrayed in Scripture as the cosmic Christ. He ascends *"far above all heavens"* (Ephesians 4:10) and *"by him all things consist"* (Colossians 1:17). At the name of Jesus *"every knee should bow, of things in heaven, and things in earth, and things under the earth; And that every tongue should confess that Jesus Christ is Lord..."* (Philippians 2:10, 11). Believers are boldly declared to be *"heirs of God"* and *"joint-heirs with Christ"* (Romans 8:17). As God's sons, believers have family authority (Galatians 4:7). We are instructed to *"Ask, and it shall be given you"* (Matthew 7:7).

The fact of the believer being ushered into the world of the supernatural, the miraculous, and the transcendent is often controversial. Because this phenomenon seems to lack logic, faith and the working of the gifts of the Spirit can appear "messy." All spiritual experience has a very real, logic-defying, mystical element and cannot always be cognized. Many spiritual experiences come, not first through cognition, but rather, through affection. For *we know not what we should pray for as we ought,* declares Apostle Paul.

> *"...but the Spirit itself maketh intercession for us with groanings which cannot be uttered."*   Romans 8:26

> *"For he that speaketh in an unknown tongue speaketh...unto God: for no man understandeth him; howbeit in the spirit he speaketh mysteries."*
> 1 Corinthians 14:2

As is the case in any true "knowing" between living, sentient beings, scripture reveals that one experiences God subjectively. The believer enters a world of knowledge, understanding, and power that is vastly larger than himself. He stands at the edge of the yawning abyss and understands only in bits and pieces. It is, nevertheless, the authentic world of the infinite and eternal. It is the world of the deep in which knowledge comes unbidden. The knowledge is "real" knowledge. However, the method of transmission is often unusual to the uninitiated.

The person praying "in the Spirit" does genuinely encounter and commune with the real, true, and living God. It is not some catatonic state induced by emotional overload. Emotional dysfunction is in no wise the same as spiritual communion with God. Equating divine, spiritual encounter with emotional excess is the common defense of those who lack such encounters. They do not know. They have never been there. These people are precisely the ones who Apostle Paul is referencing when he speaks of those who *"...occupieth the room of the unlearned"* (1 Corinthians 14:16). Thus, maybe those who do not traffic in such things should "go to their room."

Praying in the Spirit

The New Testament discussion of speaking in other tongues as the Spirit gives utterance or "praying in an unknown tongue" is, somewhat surprisingly, given a prominent role in spiritual formation. Scripture reveals valid reasons for praying in an unknown tongue, and they are very much connected to being an effective leader. Apostle Paul gives us these reasons, the first of which is, *"He that speaketh in an unknown tongue edifieth himself..."* (1 Corinthians 14:4).

This form of prayer is plainly declared to have significant benefit in personal spiritual formation. Praying in such a way strengthens, builds up, or edifies the one praying. It is not "shallow" as some wish to categorize it. Paul describes it as "praying with his spirit" and declares that it "edifies." "Edifies" comes from the Greek word *oikodomeo*, which means "to build, or to erect a structure, such as a house or temple." Philo used this same word to describe the function of the heart upon which the whole body relies and by which it is built up. Matthew 7:24 records Jesus using this same word when He tells of the man who *built* his house upon a rock (Harris, 1990). Thus, praying in tongues is at the heart of an effective, private, personal prayer life. Just as the building of one's spiritual life is likened to the building of a house or temple, the spiritual self is built up or formed from this ongoing prayer action. Praying in tongues is revealed by Paul to play a central role in the development of the individual as the house, dwelling place, or temple of the living God.

Praying in tongues provides further value to the believer in that when he prays in tongues, he is "self-instructed" by the Spirit. Fenton (1994) translates, *"The linguist instructs himself..."* Weymouth (1908) translates the verse as the one praying in this manner *"...does good to himself"* (1 Corinthians 14:4). In regards to the development of effective leadership, this mode of praying is elevated to a strategic role. Graces of the Spirit are transferred by spiritual photosynthesis from the Spirit to the individual. This is a process beyond the fumbling attempts of human logic. It is an accelerated mode of forward movement. Far from meaningless babblings, this prayer form is pregnant with unlimited potential.

While praying in tongues obviously has important value to the individual doing the praying, this is not its sole function. It is also a method whereby the Spirit of Christ intercedes through the believer for the church and the world. Paul reveals that the believer, through this kind of prayer, prays for needs of which the believer himself is not necessarily cognizant. The believer becomes an important mediatoral instrument of God. Who knows the power of a true prayer warrior to effect change! Coming through this person is world-impacting power to effect positive change. Paul explains:

> *"For if I pray in an unknown tongue, my spirit prayeth, but my understanding is unfruitful. What is it then? I will pray with the Spirit, and I will pray with the understanding also. For he that speaketh in an unknown tongue speaketh not unto men, but unto God: for no man understandeth him; howbeit in the Spirit he speaketh mysteries."*
>
> *1 Corinthians 14:14, 15, 2*

> *"...for we know not what we should pray for...but the Spirit itself maketh intercession for us with groanings*

which cannot be uttered. And he that searcheth the hearts knoweth what is the mind of the Spirit, because he maketh intercession for the saints according to the will of God." Romans 8:26,27

Here, then, are broader purposes for the biblical phenomenon of praying in tongues. First, it builds up the one praying. This alone positions it as critically important in any serious discussion of spiritual formation. Second, it is a form of instruction for the one praying. Third, such prayer is also revealed to be weighted with significance broader in scope and sweep than personal development. Individuals who pray in tongues transcend their known personal needs and even their spatial location. In a completely real but transcending way, the one praying becomes a medium of the Holy Spirit for praying for situations and/or needs universal in scope. The one praying goes beyond his/her own knowledge of what is being prayed for. *"In the Spirit he speaketh mysteries"* (i.e., secrets), Paul declares. The one praying is no longer bringing to the divine throne petitions out of his/her mind, but rather, the petitions of the Spirit's mind. Such penetrating prayer transcends conscious thought into the realm of the heavenly, the cosmic, the universal. It is evident that deep and powerful prayer plays an irreplaceably deep and powerful role in spiritual formation as well as world events.

Who knows the power of such prayer? What kind of other-worldly energies are unleashed before which no mere mortal or demonic power structure can stand? What access is provided to the believer for overcoming principalities and powers in high places? What directions, instructions, guidance, and knowledge are given to such pray-ers? Paul explains that the one praying in the Spirit speaketh "mysteries." Interestingly, *"musterion"* (Gr. mystery) often carries the idea of secrets, but more specifically, secrets revealed to those who are brought into some inner place. Through transcendent prayer, the believer is brought into previously hidden knowledge. He may receive information not available to him through personal channels of reason or communication, but only through spiritual revelation. "Secret" wisdom is given to him. While this sounds fantastic and other-worldly, and while, historically, charlatans have attempted to exploit this possibility for personal gain, Paul is, nevertheless, unequivocal in his declaration of these things.

> *"Howbeit we speak wisdom...yet not the wisdom of this world...But we speak the wisdom of God in a mystery, even the hidden wisdom, which God ordained before the world unto our glory."*   *1 Corinthians 2: 6, 7*

Scripture further states that this wisdom is derived through revelation, and, as such, is unavailable to the unbelieving world.

> *"...eye hath not seen, nor ear heard, neither have entered into the heart of man, the things which God hath prepared for them that love him. But God hath revealed them unto us by his Spirit: for the Spirit searcheth all things, yea, the deep things of God. Now we have received, not the spirit of the world, but the spirit which is of God; that we might know the things that are freely given to us of God."*
>
> *1 Corinthians 2: 9, 10, 12*

Apostle Paul clearly sees the ambiguity involved in such religious exercises as described above. He recognizes that the believer, when in such a posture of worship or prayer or praise is, in effect, suspended between two worlds: the physical and the spiritual, the material and the immaterial, the earthly and the heavenly. He admits that, even at best, we *"see through a glass darkly,"* or *"know in part"* (1 Corinthians 13). Thus, knowing that actions based on inner experience and motivation are difficult for the subject to objectively judge, he establishes a number of checks and balances such as, *"Let the prophets speak two or three, and let the other judge"* (1 Corinthians 14:29), *"...the spirits of the prophets are subject to the prophets"* (1 Corinthians 14:32), and finally, *"Let all things be done decently and in order"* (1 Corinthians 14:40).

A Little More on "Form"

The idea of "form," from which we derive "formation," is further explained in the New Testament. Given physical form at birth, further development results as a process of experience. Likewise, one is not spiritually born fully formed. As mentioned earlier, Paul emphasizes that praying in tongues edifies the believer. We have seen that "edify" is the English word chosen to translate the Greek word *oikodomeo*, which means "to build, or to erect a structure, such as a house or temple." Spiritual formation is a process of building, but it is a process triggered by a history-violating, spiritual event.

Construction does not begin with a hammer, a saw and an activity. It starts, rather, with revelation of a need and a vision of how to meet the need. Someone envisions what should be built on a bare parcel of land. In the world of the earthly, construction of the vision is then translated to paper on which is drawn the plan or pattern that the wise builder will follow. The set of plans is not the building; it is the invisible vision of the building transposed to paper. Quality plans note every important detail, large or small. Depending on the size of the building, this process often requires considerable time. Many building contractors estimate that fully one-half of the project is completed when the footings are poured. From this, the actual building process begins. First, the ground must be cleared and leveled. (Ironically, "leveling the ground" is the same metaphor used by John the Baptist to illustrate a spiritual change in the heart of man.) Digging follows clearing, then comes placing of the footings and foundation. Jesus aptly emphasizes the necessity of strong foundations. The building must be "rooted and grounded in truth." Everything depends on the correctness of these first things. It is true that the house can continue to be built even if the foundation is faulty and, when it is finished, the appearance may be fine. However, the eventual results will be, at best, weaknesses to contend with, and at worst, disastrous as the house crumbles in on its inhabitants.

Jesus teaches that every house will be exposed to pressures from every angle. The wind pressures horizontally from all the sides. The rain provides pressures from above and gathering waters create flood pressures from beneath. There is no escape. No subterfuge can provide an exit and no dodging or adroit maneuvers can avert the inevitable test. The only solution is genuine strength of construction. Simply, the house must be greater than the storm. Impermeable to nature's fury, the roof defies the rain and the foundation scoffs at the forces brought to bear against it. The center holds and the walls resolutely refuse to go down.

> *"And the rain descended, and the floods came, and the winds blew, and beat upon that house; and it fell not; for it was founded upon a rock...whosoever heareth these sayings of mine, and doeth them, I will liken him unto a wise man, which built his house upon a rock."*   *Matthew 7:24-25*

In contrast, the roof of the house built upon the sand is penetrated by the rain. Soggy weakness sets into the structure and the walls are penetrated by ruinous winds. Everything valuable within is blown away. Floods attack the weakened structure, leaving the inhabitants exposed to powerful forces of destruction. Floods wash out the sandy foundation, and the once proud house, which looked much like the other before being tested, is in ruins. Forces arrayed against the house have won.

Watching this happen to a leader is a terrifying thing, for such forces attack the foundation and structure of all leaders. These forces are conscienceless like brute beasts and they destroy totally without remorse.

Christ's use of houses as a metaphor is a clear parallel to one's life and work (cp. Matthew 7:24, 26). In His discussion of a house, He redefines the source of the assault on the house from natural forces to spiritual forces. Christ's rebuke to demons and His rebuke to forces of nature are strikingly similar (cp. Mark 4:39; 5:8). Further, He reveals that since His own house is strong, He is, in turn, on the offensive and is intent on pillaging and dismantling the devil's house. Christ is the One who is entering the "strong man's house" (i.e., Satan) and binding him, then spoiling his house (Mark 3:27). There is a violent aspect to Christ's ministry, directed not toward mankind, but toward hostile spiritual forces. No matter how "high" or how "deep" these forces may be entrenched, none of these can separate the believer from victory (Romans 8:37-39).

The above discussion reemphasizes the idea of spiritual formation as the construction of a house or temple, a "form-ed" structure to be home to the Spirit. This structure is constantly being subjected to violent opposing forces as that which holds the "Spirit-life." This structure, like any temple, is a well-ordered place out of which a ministry of healing and deliverance is expected to flow. It is a place "fitly framed" out of which blessings can flow.

Even though deep spiritual formation is a prerequisite to powerful, ongoing ministry and leadership, the process is never finished. One beholds the glory of the Lord and is changed *"from glory to glory"* and *"from faith to faith"* (2 Corinthians 3:18; Romans 1:17) and experiences *"grace heaped upon grace"* (John 1:16). Christ is not formed once and for all within a person at spiritual birth. Paul pleads, *"My little children, of whom I travail in birth again until Christ be formed in you..."* (Galatians 4:19). To the Romans he commands, *"...be ye trans-formed by the renewing of your mind"* (Romans 12:2). Indeed, as heirs of Him who has conquered death and ascended to Heaven, we are a people with a cosmic connection and heavenly history.

Going Still Deeper in the Discussion of Form and Formation
(For those who are interested)

To "be" is equivalent to having some kind of form. In life, the loss of form is the loss of being. Everything human is impelled toward form. Even the act of thinking moves toward form. We "conceptualize" or form opinions, ideas, etc., in our mind. The intellect grasps and shapes the things we encounter. With our minds, we observe things "in-form-ation," which, of course, is why "news" is called "in-form-ation," (i.e., as it happens). To "create" is to bring into formation the object that has already been formed in the thinker's mind (cp., John 5:19). This process of formation entails change, growth, and becoming. The individual life moves out from its center in an attempt to embrace and become at-one with the universe about it. There is a drive outward. While life is from within, it nevertheless is part of a context and cannot be apart from it. The integration of the self with the greater "uni"-verse is accomplished by this going out. One develops as an individual to the extent that one goes out and becomes one with God (vertical) and the human community (horizontal). This helps us to see that one simply cannot "stay within oneself" and be healthy, much less have effective ministry and leadership. To go out is to be vulnerable. Risk is involved. Courage is required. Life is not static. It is the opposite of fixedness. It is extremely dynamic, at times appearing even chaotic to both the subject and the observer. This is also true in the realm of development of human spirituality.

An example of misunderstanding such change in the spiritual realm is one psychotherapist's diagnosis of the prophet Ezekiel as "suffering from temporal lobe epilepsy, with symptoms such as extreme piety, fainting, compulsive writing, frequent inability to speak, aggression, and delusions." Ezekiel may or may not have agreed that that is how it felt to be under the anointing of God. It is doubtful that he would be concerned about the opinion of some psychotherapist unacquainted with the world of prophetic anointing. The fact is, Ezekiel, like the other prophets, in a transcendent visionary state could see and repeatedly predict the future in startling parallels to other prophets he had never met. Formation, even in the forming, conceptualizing, or articulating of thought in an anointed prophetic mode, is change. Change, in turn, creates anxiety and is therefore not easily accepted by the human mind, which tends toward seeking security in the familiar and static. Thus, prophets experienced ecstasy as well as wrenching trauma as they observed things in the Spirit that were often in stark contrast to the continuum of everyday life of which they were a part. The initial conceptualization of what they were mandated to speak thus sparked change in the speakers before their first utterance. To conceptualize something in the mind that has been given by the Spirit is to receive revelation. The act itself of receiving revelation begins a formative change in the recipient. The fact that revelatory truth is often at odds with the present circumstances of the hearer is part of the reason for its often jolting nature, and is also at least part of the reason for the persecution that often accompanies the prophet's proclamation. There is no divine manifestation that does not also carry with it judgment on that which resists its arrival. There is either blessing or judgment. There is no neutrality where prophetic anointing manifests itself.

In every human is the "possibility of being." In fact, when we are born, this potentiality is basically all there is to us. Potentiality is not a "thing" as such, but neither can it be termed complete "nothingness." As long as it remains dormant, it is equal to nothing. Nevertheless, it is not nothing, but is better described as the latent state of possibility which lies in every human being.

This subject is an important one that has occupied the minds of thinkers for centuries. It is core to an understanding of the very nature of being. The potential in every human is, in reality, the potentiality for increased being–an increase which is non-existent until one's potential is activated. This is the process that brings real form out of the "nothingness-of-potential."

Choosing to start, or accept, the process of bringing spiritual form out of one's potential is an act of the will and requires courage–courage to act, to decide, to choose, to emerge. *Thinking,* or *conceptualization,* is the beginning process of formation in the mind. Thinking leads to the formation of conclusions, and following that is *speaking,* or forming the thought into audible words. The spoken word, whether negative or positive, is more than simple articulation, but contains its own formative content (Romans10:8). The mere act of speaking carries power to move what is spoken towards self-fulfillment. Speaking carries with it a faith and an act of the will, and this faith carries the thought and spoken word toward a consummation in visible, concrete reality. This consummation of formation is grounded in the thinking and the speaking, but comes to objective reality by the power of the faith of the thinker/speaker. This faith, while invisible, is, nevertheless, in itself, also a very real thing that carries with it the power to create.

The fact that something finally becomes formed does not mean that it loses its potential to continue to create form.

Potential has a dynamic quality that continues to abide within the thing formed after it has become formed. For example, on the surface it may appear that a sculpture formed first in the mind of the sculptor, then in concrete form, becomes completely "formed" and is no longer a thing of "potential." However, because of the dynamic nature of potential, the sculpture, even though it is an inanimate object, continues to fulfill its potential on an ongoing basis as observer after observer receives the same intellectual and emotional impact that the creator received when he first conceptualized it in his mind. Thus, sculptures, paintings, written works, prayers—all of these continue to, in various ways, contain their potential to impact and create change long after their initial formation. Herein lies the secret of the priestly work of Christ. Though done once centuries ago, it continues to remain the active agent of salvation due to its continuing dynamism. What He did once *"...when he offered up himself"* (Hebrews 7: 27) continues to give life because it continues to contain the dynamism of its own potential, and thus continues to exert its liberating and ameliorating work in the world without the least weakening. Seminal things do not originate from human thought, but rather, are first found in the *tohu va bohu,* the night, the void, the darkness that precedes creation, out of which form emerges (Genesis 1:2).

What is formed out of one's potential is frequently influenced to a significant degree by environment. These influences are frequently used as the basis by which an individual makes judgments regarding their own formative actions. As a result, the critical functions of teaching, training, and exposure to that which produces positive formation, as well as exposure to the interior work of the Spirit, are of vast importance. The end goal is that everything moves outward toward a rising above its existing self and toward the creation of new forms, while at the same time preserving its own basic center as the basis for this ongoing transcendence. In other words, going out from and transcending one's present self through positive spiritual formation does not sacrifice one's identity, but rather, strengthens and reinforces it. Paul's exhortation in Romans 12:2 parallels this line of thought: *"...be not conformed to this world: but be ye transformed (Gr., transformed or transfigured by a supernatural change) by the renewing of your mind..."* To be "con-formed" is to cease the growth process, to acclimate to the world's status quo. Thus, man's thoughts, speech, and acts are capable of uniting his potential with his being to produce an ongoing, perpetual process of becoming.

An understanding of the above leads to an abundance of possibilities. First, to resist personal growth is to resist continuing to be a "being," for one either moves outward to participate and grow or regresses and eventually experiences the self-destruction of folding in on oneself. The direction of life is upward and outward, and the ultimate goal of every human life is to universalize itself, that is, to the degree possible, to embrace and become one in understanding and unity with God and His universe. To the degree one exhibits courage and determination, one goes out from oneself and learns, experiences, and develops healthy relationships with one's world. However, as previously noted, this going out is not without risks. One becomes vulnerable to the unknown. Thus, a word of caution is in order. One who naively decides to "leap out" and attempts to artificially create a "primary spiritual event instant" without guidance can bring self-destruction by losing one's "personal center" or personal identity as a being. Also, one can go out "too far" or go out in the wrong direction (e.g., the prodigal son) and not be able to get back to the subjective center of oneself. Other things can overpower the self and destroy this center, causing one to become merely another object. (The difference between a subject, such as a human being, and an object, such as a rock, is that a subject has a center of being, whereas an object has little or no center.) The ultimate perversion of nature is to turn a human subject into an object. Herein lies the sin of slavery, oppression, self-abuse, or abuse of other human beings in any and all forms.

This all has serious implications for leaders. Leaders can lead people too far too fast, or leaders can, due to their own fearfulness, be too cautious and not boldly lead people into their own potential, both corporately and individually. Just as it takes courage for the individual to venture out from his/her own personal center, it likewise requires courage of leaders to lead followers out into the greater world of challenge and opportunity. This is true spiritually as well as in life in general.

The above also has implications for *how* a leader reaches the goals God has shown him. For true leaders, "ends" never justify the use of any "means." The corporate goals of a leader–even goals given by God–never justify a leadership style that requires the turning of human "subjects" into "objects." There is no spiritual goal in which God allows the de-humanization of humans. Humans are *imago dei,* made in God's image. As a result, godly leaders cannot resort to force or violation of the human will to accomplish their goals. Such "means" automatically destroy the ends. If the leader's anointing and prophetic utterances do not carry the day, then the day is not carried. It is precisely because God rigidly abides by this precept in His own "leadership" that people will be in Hell. He does not coerce. He will not destroy the subjective center of the individual (the locus of the will) even if it would seemingly be in the individual's best interest. This is what it means to be made in God's image. Understanding the above sheds new light on the central role that submission and obedience play in spiritual formation.

Submission to God is not the equivalent of losing one's individual center. It is just the opposite. Submission to God elevates and strengthens the individual. Submission to God forbids the destruction of the individual's center, along with its attendant responsibilities. The prodigal son asks to come back home and simply be as one of the mindless, obedient servants. Though the father is joyful because of his return, he nevertheless steadfastly refuses to allow his son to return home under the aegis of an abdication of his identity as "son." In effect, the father says, "You may have left home in the first place because of your terror of emerging to accept the responsibilities of sonship. You may have sought to lose your subjective center in surfeiting and destroy it in a drunken fog. You may have had, and may still have, an enormous lack of self-confidence and of courage. Nevertheless, to come home, you are still a son. Nothing has changed." The father's act of placing the ring on the prodigal's finger is not about jewelry, but about authority and responsibility. The signet ring substitutes for signing one's signature. To have the signet ring is to have the authority and responsibility of the father himself. There is no spiritual leadership without acceptance of the responsibilities and attendant burdens that are concomitant to being God's called (Luke 1:12, 13).

As long as man preserves his status as a being with a center, he can transcend virtually any situation. Though basically finite (i.e., boundaried by the constraints of time, space, substance, and cause), he can, nevertheless, transcend his own finite boundaries. Through his mind, he can transcend limitations of place and time (e.g., he can think beyond the spot upon which he stands). On an even wider scale, the believer can, through the spirit/Spirit, transcend himself without limits in any and all directions. His potentiality in prayer and faith and action can shatter the constraints of the physical domain and reach levels never attainable on a solely natural level. *"In the world ye shall have tribulation: but be of good cheer; I have overcome the world"* (John 16:33). Through prayer, the believer breaks through the power of the finite. Also, through gifts of the Spirit, the finite is transcended. "In the Spirit," Jesus sees Nathaniel under the fig tree, sees Zacheaus in the sycamore tree, knows which fish has a coin in its mouth, knows where to find a donkey to ride on, etc. These are but a few of the biblical examples of the liberation from finite constraints that are available to the believer.

This gives heightened meaning to Paul's use of the term "word of faith." We have already observed that Christ always "saw" what He was supposed to do before He did it. This is what it means to be "led of the Spirit." The Spirit reveals the mind, or will, of God in each given situation. A Spirit-led person is shown what to do and what to speak. This is the beginning of the formation that derives from the Creative Word. The words being uttered, or the actions being taken, are Spirit-activated words or actions that take the form already in the mind of the anointed one and issue them forth into the world outside of self. These words or actions then give the conceptualization further form and move it outward through language into the world in which the predicted change becomes actualized (miracles, prophecy, etc.). Grounded in the creative nature of God as given through His Creative Word (which, in concrete form, is Jesus Christ), faith is the active ingredient in bringing the thing seen in the Spirit into authentic reality in the visible world. What was originally a thought, a vision, a dream, a perception, becomes a living Word uttered forth which, in turn, literally causes to be created the thing that was before only a possibility, a potentiality, a thought, or a vision. The anointed one literally partners with God in acts of creation!

This is, indeed, so profound that some will consider it folly. So be it. This is how spiritual power works. This is how truly "apostolic" churches are built. This is the secret ingredient in successful gospel work. What is it? See the challenge through God's eye. Then speak to the mountain which has you buried, and command it to be cast into the sea! PREACH! Preach what God has shown to you that is to be! Preach what your faith sees! Preach to your business! Preach God's promises! Preach what the Bible states! Preach to specific needs! Preach to empty pews as though they are full! Have the ushers be sure and go to each pew during the offering and "pass the plate" even though there is nobody on the last 10 pews! As a pastor, welcome everyone and be thankful for the "full house." Thank God for the powerful revival that you are having, whether or not it has happened yet. It is not a game. It is not a lie. Let God's Word put faith in you for your spouse, for your children, for your job, for your life, for your city. It is not the power of positive thinking. It is not silliness. It is faith in God's Word and faith that you have heard God's Word (read Ezekiel 37!!). Find the mind of God in prayer, in the Bible, in counsel, and then preach it!!!!!! It takes courage. It takes tenacity. It takes a firm belief that God is not a liar and that if "it" is not happening yet, it is going to as you continue to hold fresh your God-given vision and form it into words and actions until it does become healing in bodies, salvation in souls, people on pews, successful businesses, saved loved ones, transformed lives, and more. PREACH!

Chapter 5

Biblical Models of Greatness Emerging from the Deep

The Old Testament, as well as the New, repeatedly uses water metaphorically to signal a "cross-over" point in the life-development of great leaders. There is a "before" and "after" portrait of each. The "before" is prior to the primary spiritual event instant in the lives of individuals. It reveals their character and actions prior to being confronted by and/or plunged into the deep, while the "after" reveals the differences in them subsequent to their plunge. Some go through willingly while others appear to be driven there by circumstances. Nevertheless, all who experience greatness go. A few appear to be virtually dragged there kicking and resisting. One (Jonah) is literally thrown headlong into the deep. The "before" and "after" difference in each of the following examples is radical and shocking. While the circumstances vary greatly in their personal spiritual development, the overall pattern is startlingly consistent. Greatness demands taking the journey, leaving the familiar, and stepping away from seeming stability and security onto the always-rocking platform of life on the fluid. To use another metaphor mentioned earlier, when these leaders come to the "gate," they do not mill about, but rather, they press resolutely forward into the frontier of the unexplored, the deep, the unknown world. The record of virtually every great biblical leader reveals this connection to the deep.

Noah
and the Baptism of the Earth

That Noah's experience truly has meaning for spiritual formation in terms of "going to the deep" is seen in that the inundation of his day is likened unto baptism in the New Testament (1 Peter 3:20, 21).

One aspect of "going to the deep" that we do not deal with in any of the other following examples is seen clearly in Noah's encounter. It is perhaps the first and foremost aspect of change brought about by the deep destruction of and radical separation from one's personal past. We will look at the typological implications of four primary results of the flood. The flood event simultaneously reveals failure and provides hope. It also reveals the divine method for making that hope available.

Noah's arrival on the biblical scene comes early in man's history. As it relates to spiritual formation, the flood plunges both Noah and the earth into the deep. Ironically, the earth was formed out of the deep. Now formed, the earth itself has begun to produce life. On the surface of the earth's form (i.e., dry land), new form is taking place by way of plants, animals, and human life. However, this process of formation has become grossly twisted. The formation that was orderly and beautiful is now spastic and horribly distorted. Man, the most refined of that which was formed, is now hopelessly perverted. To God, this is not simply about man going astray, but the whole process of earth formation going astray. The remarkable thing about the Noah narrative is that it is not just about an individual going to the deep, but rather, the entire earth being re-enveloped in the darkness of the deep. Thus, God declares:

"...I will destroy man whom I have created from the face of the earth; both man, and beast, and the creeping thing, and the fowls of the air..." Genesis 6:7

The fact that man has gone astray indicts the whole of creation and, except for the occupants of the ark, plunges the earth back into the primordial state of Genesis 1:2. Even so, the preservation of Noah and the fact of the eventual receding of the waters reveals that the divine purpose of judgment is not punishment for its own sake, but a manifestation of the resolve and intent of God for creation to fulfill its potential.

Just as the first thing revealed is what transpires when potential is perverted (i.e., judgment, hope, and a new start), the second observation is how thorough is the cutting off of that which has twisted into grotesque malformation. Proper formation is so central to natural order that, when it ceases, earth dramatically sinks once again into lifeless, prehistoric silence. In tandem with this, mankind, formed from dust of the earth, is also utterly re-submerged in the deep of judgment (Genesis 7:22, 23). Rather than rise once again from the "loins of the earth," man will be formed through the rescue of grace, of which Noah is the personification (Genesis 6:8). Now, not only man, but the whole future of all life on earth can be found only in the grace (enablement) that floats above judgment and transcends the violent collapse of formation from beneath. Henceforth, all formation will derive from the seed that transcends judgment and death. All of this, of course, prefigures Christ who is "from above," who brings hope through the administration of God's grace.

It also should not be forgotten that Noah and the flood is likened to Christian baptism. The one baptized is violently separated from his/her old life, which is submerged forever in the deep. This separation from the "old man" is radical and unequivocal. Often to the degree that the understanding of the significance and importance of baptism is lacking, this cutting off of the old life is also lacking.

Not only is there a thorough separation from yesterday's lifestyle, but there is also a decisive death to yesterday's goals, aspirations, and interests. *"...buried with him by baptism"* (Romans 6:4) is more than a catch-phrase. That which rises from the watery grave (cp. Genesis 1:2) of baptism rises from the deep to be the seed of Christ, who is "the man of grace who rides above judgment." This is literally a new birth of a new man.

This process of spiritual formation, which forms a new man, culminates in a new focus and a new understanding of one's identity and purpose. Noah is no longer just "another man," but comes out of the flood with a divine mandate so broad that the future of earth itself is tied directly to his fulfillment of God's purpose. His importance can hardly be overemphasized.

The gravity with which ministers treat their ministry is tied directly to this understanding, that is, their importance and the importance of the message given to them to declare to the world. It is leadership on a universal level. One so anointed may be assigned to some small and remote post of duty. It doesn't matter, for leadership actions of one so anointed will transcend the context in which they are carried out and will expand far beyond the immediate time and place.

Jacob
—Showdown at Sundown

Twenty miles upstream from the Dead Sea, the River Jabbok flows from the east into the River Jordan. Jacob has traveled across Jordan, found his wife and prosperity, and is now returning home. Here, located halfway between the Dead Sea and living Galilee, a man is caught between life and death. A wily man who has always finagled his way, Jacob is confident in himself, his skills, and his accomplishments. He knows he is destined to be a great patriarch. However, he does not know what it is going to require. He is successful, but God wants greatness. Attaining such greatness will require transformation of his defective character and will be exacting in the deep areas of his inner man. Involving the interior self more than skills or knowledge, this development will require exploring motives, manifesting courage, and developing a respect for justice and truth that he presently doesn't have. He will learn that right must reign over expedience. Perhaps he has long forgotten his past deviousness. Or perhaps for these years he has attributed his character flaws to the genes he inherited from his mother, who clearly had the same character. He may view himself as a fated victim of a generational curse, and therefore dismiss his deficiencies as someone else's fault. It is true that others have rationalized their actions with such logic, but because he is a child of destiny, he cannot. He is a fated leader leading a fated people. They are God's people and they are great in the sight of the Lord. As their leader, he must model the way. Once a deal-maker, politician, and consummate grabber of whatever is before him, Jacob is finally discovering that though he may experience temporary "success," this is not God's way. In God, the means are as important as the ends, and the journey is an inextricable part of the destination. Process and product are inseparable. Being technically proficient is not the same as being biblically great. True greatness in leadership allows no disconnect between "being" and "doing."

In meeting God, Jacob also meets his past and his character defects. It is unavoidable. He has done others wrong. As with many others, it appears for years that he has "gotten by" with this. Many of the incidents are long forgotten. Enjoying the fruits of success, the past seems far away. Now having come full circle, he is returning to the land of promise as a leader. Excited? Certainly. But does he understand that leaders imprinted with destiny also have divine demands laid upon them? Does he know that the divine One will take him on a Spirit-journey of exploration into the deep and dark places within himself and within his call? He is about to discover that divine demands are layered much deeper than human craftiness. And does he know that if he fails this test and is still thrust into leadership, the results will be a destructive imprint both upon him as well as those who follow him? Like all before and after him, he will plunge, or be plunged, into the deep and the dark. He will not escape meeting the foreboding and the unseen personally before he meets it as the leader of God's people.

Words such as "foreboding" and "terrifying" and "deep and dark places" are appropriate descriptors that match well the descriptions of the journey found in Psalm 107. There will almost certainly be those who think the use of such words to be inappropriate. They will attempt to lighten the discussion of spiritual formation to safer, less threatening ground. Others will go so far as to hold such ideas in derision. Nevertheless, the shallower the waters of formation, the fewer the wonders of the Lord will be seen. The wonderful, the powerful, the glorious, are in the deep. For those who have never been "there," and have no intention of going, explanation is futile. For those who have been there, it is unnecessary. For those who desire to go, it is available, but only at a price. Salvation is free: greatness in leadership is not. Jacob can get at the greatness that lies in his potential only by passing through the deep and wrestling with himself and with God.

There are several striking points in this story that form a motif, which is found repeatedly both here and in other scriptural accounts of leadership development.

First, *Jacob comes to the water.* Darkness is upon the water. This dark water is the divider between desire and fulfillment, between potential and concrete reality, between one's present and one's destiny. Only by entering the water and crossing to the other side can he arrive at the place that will resonate with and receive his ministry.

It is night. There are things that do not happen in daylight. They are reserved for the night. The sun of prosperity may shine upon one for an extended period of time. However, times of intense, "no turning back" spiritual formation invariably partner with the night. Darkness is upon the face of the water with the entire scene shrouded in eeriness. Jacob wrestles in the dark. Jacob is "in the dark." The future is not clear. The dangers are real. In the form of Esau, his earlier actions of achieving the birthright through trickery and without sufficient spiritual formation now threaten his very life. This is a dark time for Jacob in more ways than one.

"...Jacob was left alone..." (Genesis 32:24). In example after example of deep spiritual formation, the called one is found alone. Constant social interaction can enable one to avoid introspection. With all of the important and necessary positives associated with being active in one's larger community, this is one place that is a sure exception. Surfeiting on the inviting and familiar places of life prevents the kind of inward confrontations that deep spiritual formation requires.

Life in our hurried world has created an aversion to being alone. Chattering voices and flickering images pervade life with new inventions and contrivances whereby one is "kept in touch." The fear of loneliness is real. However, while technology can mask this aloneness, it cannot resolve it.

Being an individual carries with it this separateness from all others. It is a characteristic of being finite. The answer lies not in attempting to escape the reality of loneliness, but in turning this aloneness into solitude—that is, a peaceful state of acceptance of God's order and intimacy with God. To do so, however, one must first encounter God and His purpose for his/her life. Once this happens, loneliness, which was a negative, is transformed into positive solitude. This solitude is a source of strength and peace. It is being "at one" with oneself, with God, with God's will, and with the ultimate order of things.

This night has been a long time in coming for Jacob, but now it has finally and irreversibly arrived. This night is a culmination of many events. Jacob is wealthy. He is successful. He is crafty. But he is defective. In essence, God is saying, "Yes, Jacob, come on. Indeed, great promises have been given to you and you are integral to my plan. But first, you must, of necessity, be re-formed and trans-formed." Jacob is about to discover that there are aspects of life that transcend human control. He will face the reality of his duplicity in ways that he never dreamed. Esau is coming to meet him with 400 men. Jacob is terrified, and rightly so, for the last we have heard from Esau, his intention was to slay Jacob in revenge for the stolen blessing (Genesis 27:41, Gaebelein, 1990). Further, he has taken the best of Laban's herds. He is a schemer, a man who has carefully out-planned and out-smarted every opponent, including his own father. But now there is no escape. God has caught up with him. Planning as always, he lays out an elaborate scheme to pacify Esau. However, with Jordan still to cross, his options are exhausted. God has Jacob where He wants him. It has taken a very long time to maneuver him into this position, but now he is here and he will not escape.

"...and there wrestled a man with him..." (Genesis 32: 24). Wrestling is perhaps the most strenuous of all physical action. There is no pretty and delicate posturing here and no place for aloof intellectual musings. There is a place where one should be able to exist with fragility, but this is not it. Jacob's wrestling is a spiritual struggle too awful to describe. He is dying, and his name is dying with him. Driven beyond rationality, he will cease to be or else become a new man with a new name. There is no in-between. Life cannot continue as before. It is a struggle beyond strength, beyond athleticism, beyond skill. All is reduced to its simplest form. The struggle is elemental. The body, exerted beyond thought or strategy, doggedly fights on and resists hour after hour by mere desperation and grit of mind and will. Locked by the angel in silent, deadly combat, Jacob fights on through the night. Every trick is used and fails. Every feint, every subterfuge is countered. Jacob clearly wants to escape. He did not ask for this confrontation. He has always been able to wiggle out. But his wiliness has met its match. The angel will brook no talk of quitting, of escape, of truce. The time has come. He will look God in the eye. Jacob will look himself in the eye. He will look Esau in the eye.

"...and He touched the hollow of his thigh; and the hollow of Jacob's thigh was out of joint" (Genesis 32:25). What a contrast between entry and exit! Jacob's walk will be forever different. Not only different, but in a noticeable way—a way that marks him as one who has wrestled with God. For Jacob, the mark is physical, but the didactic intent of this verse clearly is to illustrate that those who have wrestled in such places are easy to identify in public. They walk differently. They are different. They have a holy crippledness. While becoming exceptionally strong, they are aware that they are exceptionally weak.

"...Let me go, for the day breaketh" (Genesis 32:26). With Jacob fully absorbed in the struggle, the divine One also wrestles, but maintains awareness of the larger picture. He is aware that there are time limits to this kind of confrontation. It is not an everyday occurrence. He knows that this stage of spiritual formation comes at select times and that tonight

is the night. Now, if the work cannot be accomplished in that specific period, then life must move on, divine business elsewhere calls. Life is not static. Jacob will be the loser. The moments of this night have been counted and stamped and reserved in Heaven for this encounter. The bout is timed. If there is no victory this night, then it is over. "Daybreak" is the bell that will end the match. There will be no extensions.

"Wrestled...until the breaking of the day" (Genesis 32: 24). The question arises as to why the struggle took all night. Why did Jacob have to wait so long to be blessed? Why not just "claim it" and move on? The answer seems to be that there were actually two wrestling matches going on—one with self and one with God. All through the night Jacob hangs onto not the angel, but self. In contrast, the angel wrestles to pry Jacob from self, from old ways, etc. Finally, the angel quits. It's morning. Forget it. Time is up. Jacob, exhausted from his refusal to give himself up, finally realizes he is going to once and for all surrender or be left to his own devices. He grabs the angel. The angel responds, "It is too late, let go of me. You have fought against me too long." Jacob answers, "NO! I give up self, my old agenda, my own plan! I must have you!" The angel, says "No. It is too late. The sun is rising. You have resisted submission all night. These things are not done in the light. I must go." Jacob clings frantically to the angel. The grip...if he can just keep the grip...focus only on the grip! No matter what, don't let go!

Who started this fight? The language of the Bible indicates that this match was originated by the Lord. God started the fight.

> *"And Jacob was left alone; and there wrestled a man with him until the breaking of the day. And when he (i.e., the angel) saw that he prevailed not against him..."*   *Genesis 32:24-25*

It is the angel who is doing the grappling and holding through the night. It is Jacob who is attempting to escape. Just before daybreak, the angel is about to leave in defeat. He has been unable to pry Jacob from his embrace of himself, therefore he will exit without success. Jacob senses this change and finally realizes that God will no longer allow him to continue to embrace self and God simultaneously. He is at a crossroads with destiny. What a strange and terrifying experience for this self-loving man to release his lifelong self-embrace. Nevertheless, to his credit he does so and, as fiercely as he previously embraced self, he now embraces God. The angel ultimately wins. He wrestles down Jacob's rebellion. He wrestles down his defective character.

The result. The battle is over. God wins. But Jacob also wins, not over God, but over self. God commends him. He is marked, but changed—elevated. He can now be the patriarch God desires him to be. The result of this change is an inward change in Jacob. His name is also changed, signifying a very real new identity. (How many times has this name change occurred in scripture?!) He becomes "Israel." He is one who now has power with God and with man. Secondary results will follow. Oneness and unity with his brother will result. Ability to continue his journey into his destiny will result. Jacob finds a home, builds an altar and a house, and walks into the greatness God has in store for him.

Joseph
—Do Great Dreams Die Before They Live?

As we have seen, all "great" people in the Bible have a sharply defined "before" and "after" in their lives. The dividing point is consistently their coming to the "edge." In case after case, this intersection is connected with water and/or the deep. This is not a coincidence. Their encounters clearly follow the process outlined in Psalm 107. Joseph is no exception. Even he is thrown into a deep well or cistern. Joseph–the snappy dresser with the multi-colored sports coat and a head full of dreams. But blood will stain that coat as well as those dreams before they will be realized. Joseph is one of those blessed early with a vision of his destiny to lead. In tandem visions, he realizes that he will have dominion over his parents and brethren. However, having a vision and seeing the fulfillment of that vision are two vastly different things. As is the case with most who are young, Joseph, in his youth, does not realize this. He appears to be more than a little egotistical. His dreams are deep but his life is shallow. Self-superior and his father's obvious favorite, he engenders the jealousy and hatred of his brethren. In terms of his relationship with his brethren, his visions hang like a curse around his neck. His youth has not equipped him to share these visions in such a way that lifts others. They are, rather, a source of alienation. He is blessed. He is favored. He is visionary. Nevertheless, he is about to learn that all divine visions given to men must fall to the earth like a seed and die before they live. He will discover that there is a "lot of living" between visions held and visions realized. He will also discover that only "resurrected visions" find fulfillment. His visions are much greater than his current level of spiritual formation. God will "go backward" to his level of formation and bring him forward. The fulfillment of the vision depends on the results of this formational process. This process entails "going to the deep" and includes a death of both the visionary and the vision. Divine visions that come to pass are, invariably, resurrected visions. Divine visionaries are almost always resurrected visionaries.

Many important elements are included in Joseph's journey to the deep. Early on he is given an opportunity to become bitter at his brethren. Next, he is exposed to the deep, the dark, the confining. He is alone. He is, typically speaking (and almost literally), buried. Third, he is given the opportunity to lose the vision by succumbing to seduction, or, after refusing to compromise, by becoming bitter at being falsely accused and lied about for doing what is right and honorable. To match his two visions, he experiences two dungeons–the second is a jail cell in Pharaoh's prison. There he experiences being forgotten and also experiences being on the receiving end of unkept promises. Joseph represents a seed that falls into the earth and dies that it might germinate and resurrect with the wonder and mystery of new life and anointing. Only then do his visions unfold like the petals of a rose. Of a certainty, the descent of Joseph in every way equals his subsequent dramatic ascent. Actualization of his potential and fulfillment of his dreams would never have come had he not been put in the pit. It is these perilous experiences that drive to either bitter destruction or powerful leadership. The wind that drives one to shipwreck drives another to his destiny. It depends on the set of the sail. For one, the stone is a stumbling stone. For others, it is a stepping stone. Joseph is the paragon of proper response to challenges and adversity.

Jochebed and Moses
— Making Kids Hip or Holy

Who knows the full scope of the role of Moses' parents in the process of nurturing his spiritual formation? Where would Moses be without a mother who, virtually from birth, exposes him to the deep? What insight, what wisdom, what courage this woman possesses! Defiant of the mightiest political and military power in the world, she resolutely refuses to compromise her or her son's future. She doesn't hide him in the house or on land, but literally starts his life on the gently rocking waves of the deep—the Nile. She is no shrinking violet, narrow-thinking mother, nor does she shy from the challenges that her world presents to her in regards to the survival and upbringing of her son. The need is too great and times too desperate for spoiling her son with toys and the surfeiting of parental love. She knows His salvation, as well as the salvation of the nation, is dependent upon this sole act of her boldly exposing her child to the deep. It is a risk, but she well knows that long after world empires sag to decay and the whispering wind finds no inhabitants therein, only the children of the holy will continue to live and stand tall forever.

From the beginning, Moses is exposed to the deep. From early childhood, his life is beyond the ordinary and is a walk of faith. His life is sustained only by destiny and God's promises. His mother and Pharoah's daughter are juxtaposed. There is no doubt that Mother has etched core convictions deep in him. Pharaoh's daughter offers the courts of Pharaoh. Mother offers the courts of God. Pharaoh offers the world's greatest finite empire. Mother counters by leading him on a tour of the infinite. Is it any surprise, then, that he chooses the people of God over Egypt? From babyhood, faith is his lifestyle. His worldview, his way of processing life's challenges, his methods for decision-making–all arise from this seminal faith and exposure to universals. There is no earthly kingdom that can compete with such glory, such challenge, such breadth.

There is a faith lifestyle. It is a lifestyle with which the cautious and the carnal have much difficulty. History is strewn with the failures of those who came charging confidently to the precipice of the faith-life, then, terrified by the yawning abyss before them, slowly backed away. They simply lacked the faith to leap. Trembling and backpedaling, they moved away from opportunity. The faith-life was too foreign to their demand for seeming security. It is an unpleasant thing to watch one so caught literally crumble into a nervous mass of fear and terror.

A brief survey of Moses, Jacob, and Joseph reveals that all three of them are called early in life. They are gifted, and each misuses those gifts. In all three cases, a deep and traumatic confrontation with God and self takes place, which brings them to the new, powerful level of formation necessary to see the fulfillment of the visions God had given them. Prior to this encounter, and despite their best efforts, their gifts produce division, confusion, destruction, and even murder. Only when Jacob comes to Jabbok, Joseph to the pit and jail, and Moses to the burning bush do deep changes and dramatic new levels of formation begin in them. Vision "falls to the earth" and dies. Only then is it resurrected. Greatness arises out of utter death to self. The refinement is exceedingly thorough. The result is, *"not my will but Thine be done."*

Elisha
—The Tag-Along

Elisha comes from a different path to ministry than those we have already observed. He begins as a tutored servant to another's ministry. The most outstanding characteristic of Elisha's formation is his tenacious loyalty to his mentor. There are many "sons of the prophets" in the land. They are found at Bethel. They are found at Jericho. They are found following afar off. But only Elisha doggedly matches Elijah step-for-step.

Oftentimes, those who follow God closely seem to find themselves at odds with God. God Himself seems to attempt to pry them away from this intimacy. In this case it is Elijah who, at every turn, discourages Elisha. Is this intentional? Is this a test? What is the motive? Elijah attempts to leave him in Gilgal while he goes to Bethel, then attempts to leave him in Bethel as he goes to Jericho. At Jericho, Elijah encourages Elisha to stay while he continues to Jordan. In the meantime, the other sons of the prophets also seem to discourage him at every turn and attempt to pry him loose from Elijah. Through all of this, Elisha remains patient, determined, and faithful to Elijah. He refuses to be pried away from close proximity to Elijah until Elijah is finally taken up. Elisha is rewarded with his mantle.

Much can and should be said about loyalty to one's mentor or father-in-spiritual-formation. For many, this seems to be a hard lesson to learn. Young, impatient, and filled with a false confidence that fools him into thinking he is are already beyond his elders, many is the young prophet who has been careless in his treatment of and respect for his mentor. Every young prophet is given the chance to be an opportunist—grabbing every chance for self promotion and ministry without considering the "macro" picture. Short-term gains are appealing but do not reveal their cost until much later.

This temptation to disdain one's mentor seems to come to most upcoming leaders. Like a teen chafing at parental controls, it sometimes seems the elder has become too slow and is no longer "cutting edge." Impatience easily turns to criticism and criticism to disregard. However, the wise stay close, knowing that the mantle is all that matters.

Elisha's story also teaches us that the anointing is not something new. There is a clear transfer pattern discernible throughout both the Old and the New Testaments. From Moses, anointed leadership is passed to Joshua. We also see this in the monarchy, from Saul to David and from David to Solomon. After Solomon, the mistake is made by assuming that the anointing can be passed down genetically. But this is not so. Each succeeding leader must be in the leader line, not by lineage, but by divine selection and appointment. When genetics is presumed to be the key in Israel, then spiritual leadership is transferred from the kings to the prophets. It is in this prophetic lineage that we find Elijah and Elisha. Anointing has been transferred from leader to leader for centuries.

So the anointing Elisha receives is, in a very real sense, transferred. It is the Spirit of God, but also the "spirit of Elijah." Without Elijah, Elisha would never have been mantled with such. It is a trust passed from anointed to anointed. The medium by which Elisha receives anointing is Elijah. Such power and enablement is not given to others, but only to God's leaders. It is unique. It is unsurpassed. No badge or uniform can equal it. No court, legislative body, or army can match it. It is supernatural. It is heavenly. "I have overcome the world," (Gr., *kosmos*) saith the Lord. There is nothing in this world as powerful as a man or woman of God anointed by the Spirit. This has been the secret of the most powerful leadership for centuries.

Elisha waits. This transfer is a sacred and holy trust. Then the day finally comes when Elijah is taken up in the whirlwind. The old prophet's mantle floats back to the earth. Generations come and go, but the need for leadership remains on the earth. Elisha picks it up. Nothing but a mantle. It is the only thing he inherits from his mentor. However, this mantle of anointing is the most influential thing in Elisha's life from this time forward. Never again will he farm or plow. His ranching days are over. He is forever marked and fated by the anointing.

Elisha's very first test of his anointing is the deep. He must cross the river to reach the locus of his ministry. Can the mantle get him through the deep? He learns that, with the prompting of God, one enters the deep of his own volition. Once he enters, however, he is exposed to the wonders of the Lord. Elisha thus begins his ministry by doing business in "great waters." His first tentative step is to use Elijah's mantle, call on Elijah's God, and expect Elijah's results. (Question: Did Elisha ever have a ministry he could call his own? Or were his dramatic results always the result of a "double portion" of Elijah's spirit? Does anyone have a ministry that is exclusively their own?) Elijah's God works. Elijah's anointing works. Elijah's power for ministry rests with Elisha. The waters are parted. Elisha doesn't need his own anointing. It is enough to have Elijah's power times two.

Jonah
—Walking the Plank

Who is this Jonah and why is he so important for the subject of formation of ministry and spirituality? Of all the biblical models in which spiritual formation takes a person into the deep, Jonah is certainly the most literal example. There is a reason for this. Jonah is a much more important character than the size of the book bearing his name may indicate. Christ uses Jonah as a type of Himself, revealing that His and Jonah's journeys to the deep parallel one another. By doing this, Christ also reinforces our belief that all of these examples are intended to be taken together to move us toward the development of a theology of spiritual formation.

Jonah harbors a strong resistance to God's call. He is fearful. He is biased and opinionated. He is prejudiced. He thinks resistance can free him from his call to spiritual leadership. However, his destiny is irrevocably intertwined with fulfilling the ministry to which God has called him. Try as he may, there is no life for him outside of obedience. He is a stalked man—stalked by the call of God. His disobedience not only jeopardizes his life personally, but the lives of those who travel with him, as well as those who hear not the message of God because of his rebellious refusal to preach. Finally, rather than step into the deep, Jonah is violently thrown into the deep.

Scholars admit surprise that the book of Jonah is even included in the canon of scripture. This surprise is not because the book contains incredible events, such as a man being swallowed by a great fish and then being cast upon the shore. Nor is it because Jonah is an embarrassment due to his disobedience. It is, rather, that Jonah is such an indicting microcosm of the failure of Israel as a nation to fulfill the mission God committed to them—that is, to be a blessing (through the preaching of the gospel) to the rest of the world.

Israel was never a people who God intended to be isolated upon the earth (Kaiser, 1978). From the first call of Abraham, God clearly identified that the reason He was blessing Abraham and his descendants was so that, through Israel, the nations of the earth could be blessed (Genesis 12:3). They were to be the transmitters of the "blessing of Abraham" to the rest of the earth. This was their purpose. While some may doubt that "missions" is found in the Old Testament, the record is emphatically clear that God's intent from the beginning was for His called-out people to take their blessing from Him and to share it with the nations of the earth. The psalmist declares:

> *"God be merciful unto us, and bless us; and cause his face to shine upon us; Selah."*   Psalm 67:1

The psalmist prays for blessing, then quickly states the reason:

> *"That thy way may be known upon earth, thy saving health among all nations."*   Psalm 67:2

The people of Israel, like Jonah, were a minority called to serve a majority. They were specifically called to be a "kingdom of priests" (Exodus 19). It was meant for them to serve in a mediatorial role between God and the world and they were meant to be set apart to God and His service. They were expected to abstain from worldly interests and focus on worldwide ministry.

Israel failed miserably in this assignment. They thought God had saved them for themselves, and failed to realize that He had saved them for His purposes and His mission. They misconstrued their blessing, their enablement, and their giftedness, and came to view others condescendingly as lesser human beings beneath their dignity. Their blessing led them to prejudice and spite. They detested the Gentile "dogs."

No one personifies this national attitude more precisely than Jonah. Called and blessed of God, he is directed to go to Nineveh, but his disdain for the Ninevites is blatant. He despises them. To him, they are unworthy of his message and incapable of obedience. He has become so fixated on self that he no longer has God's view toward the nations of the world. He maintains a resolute unsubmissiveness to the call of God. God has chosen Jonah to take His message to a city that is the epitome of Gentile power and gods. He refuses to go. Jonah is the exact opposite of an apostle. God's will is to spread the good news to the world. Jonah's will is to keep it contained within Israel alone. Jonah is the carnal man who attempts to sabotage God's worldwide plans.

To portray the depth of this rebellion, the writer of the book of Jonah uses minute details to show that the winds obey God, but not Jonah. Jonah sleeps while the world about him perishes. God can guide the wind, the sailors, and the great fish, but not Jonah. Jonah prays for deliverance. Ironically, he who refuses to take God's deliverance to the Ninevites prays for deliverance.

But Jonah is not the only one who is stubborn. God delivers him, then immediately repeats His orders. God has His own purposes. He will not let up. In the whale's belly, Jonah declares, "Yahweh is salvation." God responds by saying, "That's true. Now go tell that to the Ninevites." God resolutely insists that Jonah tell Nineveh that God is concerned about them.

Jonah is very unhappy. He finds it exceedingly distasteful that God is intending to share the blessing of Abraham with Nineveh. The book ends with Jonah obeying God resentfully and his obedience is still a subject of question. God has sent Jonah to Nineveh, the second oldest city in the world, the home of Nimrod, the home of every man-made religion and foul spirit. God has sent him there to show His universal power over all that Nineveh represents. Jonah sees the message as having a smaller sphere than this. God sees the message as powerful enough to bring down universal principality, power, and dominion. He then proceeds to prove it. His message is more powerful than the world's, even though it comes from a half-hearted prophet.

Jonah is one of those who finds going to the deep traumatic beyond words. It is doubly so for him because of his unsubmitted will. His rebellion, evidently never completely resolved, gives him a ministerial life of tumult and smoldering resentment. The deep love God has for the lost is something Jonah never grasps. He never comes to a place of ultimate trust, thanksgiving, and resignation to God and His will. God's greatest challenge is not the storm, the fish, or the Ninevites, but the unsubmitted will of the prophet. Bigoted, prejudiced, and narrow-minded, Jonah, along with the stiff-necked kings of Israel, resists God. In contrast, the most violent king, who is a heathen, along with an entire heathen city, humbles himself before the living God.

As mentioned before, Christ likens Himself to Jonah in that both go to the deep. However, in terms of understanding God's mission, the comparison between Christ and Jonah becomes a stark contrast. Whereas Jonah grows increasingly more angry that God would even extend mercy to those outside of Israel, Christ has a long list of ministry to lost Gentiles. He:

- Commends the wisdom of Sarepta, a Gentile city, at the beginning of His ministry (Luke 4);
- Delivers a Gadarene Gentile from demonism (Matthew 8:28-34);
- Heals 10 lepers, only one of which—a Samaritan—returns (Luke 17:12-19);
- Gives some of the greatest theological truths ever to a lone Samaritan woman of questionable reputation (John 4);
- Rewards the faith of a Canaanite woman by healing her daughter (Matthew 15:24);

- Gives a miracle to a Centurion, an alien commander of an alien army of occupation (Matthew 8:8, 11, 12);
- Attracts Greeks (John 12:23, 32). The deep interest of the Greeks is evidence that the world is ready to receive the good news of His redemptive mission; and
- Reiterates the purpose of the people of God to go into all the world and preach the good news (Matthew 28:19).

Certainly, a greater than Jonah is here.

Chapter 6

Jesus – The Perfect Model

No one goes more dramatically to the deep of spiritual formation than Jesus. No story, true or fictional, is more profound. His going to the deep is neither coincidental nor covert. It is an overwhelming compulsion that makes Him unconscious of all else. This "plunge" in His life takes place at His baptism. Christ is subjected to the deep in a way that being submerged in the waters of Jordan could only gesture towards. Prior to this stepping "over the edge," there is little written about Him other than a few facts about His birth and early childhood. Evidently there is little of consequence about which to write. Life at Nazareth was inconspicuous and without particularity. That is, before baptism. But upon being plunged into the deep, the picture is accelerated so rapidly and radically that it is breathtaking. (Note: For those who find it difficult to think of Christ as being truly "human" in the development of ministry, one may at least think of Christ as "modeling" leadership formation. Either way, the record clearly discloses the model for all authentic human spiritual formation that leads to truly elite leadership.)

Coming out of the baptismal waters, Jesus is literally catapulted into another sphere. For the first time, the full weight of the ultimate mandate of His destiny is laid upon Him and this before all. The force of this announcement so completely explodes His old world that He bursts from the waters as one possessed, one driven, totally overwhelmed with the enormity of what has just been revealed and activated in Him. Although He unquestionably has known from birth that He is the Son of God, nevertheless, this is a time of stupendous self-discovery of His messiahship and what it entails. He is shaken to the core of His human being. His time has come.

Immediately, Jesus is *driven* (Mark 1:12) into the wilderness where He will sort out this radical turn of events. Zeal (Gr., "to be hot, boil of liquids") eats Him up (John 2:17). However, it is not yet time to preach, but rather, to ferret out three issues that are critical to all leadership formation regardless of time, age, or place. These are identity, mission, and methods.

As evidenced in the Gospel accounts, Christ's baptism and temptation in the wilderness are the seminal events in the formation of His ministry. Before His baptism and temptation, He is simply the humble carpenter living in uninterrupted commonness. After His baptism, His life has universal impact. Before, He is subject to parents and to the limitations of culture, time, and location. After, His ministry is one of kingship and power and dominion, not only over earthly concerns but over the entire cosmos. He is hardly recognizable as the same person.

Could it be that the anointing of God is meant to so radically transform all who are genuinely called of God, regardless of the time period (Wilson, 1981)? Is it too much to expect that Christ's example should also serve as the model for every succeeding minister and leader? While such a promise at first glance appears extreme, such a conclusion, nevertheless, seems to be the clear intent of scripture. Jesus, while praying in preparation for transferring His work to His followers, declares, *"As thou hast sent me into the world, even so* (i.e., the same way) *have I also sent them into the world"* (John 17:18). "Sent as he is sent!" Though we will not trace it out here, this transfer motif is central to all Spirit-empowered leadership, whether Old Testament or New Testament. In contrast to the Pharisees, Jesus is sent "as One who has authority." There is a dynamic quality to His ministry that is other-worldly and timeless. It is a ministry that, of a certainty, does business "in great waters," and sees "the works of the Lord and His wonders in the deep" (Psalm 107:23, 24).

One might ask, how do we obtain the story of Christ's temptation? No one else is present as it unfolds. Holy Writ records that the stage for this drama includes only Christ, God, Satan, wild beasts, and angels (Mark 1:12, 13). Thus, Christ must make an effort to express it to His disciples, or else how can they write of it?

The temptation is an other-world experience which models the wrenching process of spiritual formation. The experience is high and mystical. The artist Tissot grasps the sense of it with is painting depicting Jesus borne on the fingertips of a gigantic specter. However, when the painting is observed closely, the specter is actually Jesus' own shadow.

Prior to the temptation, Jesus has little distinctive identity. Other than a few facts of His birth and the incident at twelve years of age, there is nothing. Upon emergence from the temptation, however, He lays bold and unapologetic claim to being the Messiah and the revealer of the Father. Gushing out of Him is power of such force that all is carried before it. Obviously something very great takes place during this time. To Jesus the man, the overwhelming implications of being Messiah are revealed. "Driven" of the Spirit into the wilderness, we find no gentle, logical process here or casual exploration of possibilities. It is life and death.

Three spheres of temptation are disclosed by Matthew and Luke. Each of them is applicable to all leadership development. Each is accompanied by profound revelation.

The first revelation is one of Jesus receiving, verifying, and accepting His *self-identity* as defined by God. His recurring devilish temptation is to doubt his God-given identity. *"If thou be the Son of God..."* is the repeated challenge. This deep, unshakeable awareness of who He is becomes the foundation of His ministry. Satan challenges this identity repeatedly. Family members question this identity. The religious leadership of the day goes so far as to question His sanity. Some fling the awful accusation that He is demonic. All of these attacks focus on identity. Destruction of His faith that He is called of God is tantamount to destruction of the foundation upon which His ministry is formed. This formation process begins with challenges to His call and the identity that arises from this call. It continues throughout His ministry. Finally, while on the cross, the thief one last time hurls the challenge into His face, *"If thou be the Christ..."* Throughout this formative process, Jesus is unswerving, unmoved, and fully-assured. Such a victory arising out of this wilderness encounter is experienced personally before it is made manifest in His public ministry. Victories won in private manifest themselves in public. As we have already seen, Luke redacts these events to show that, upon emerging from the temptation, Christ immediately and assuredly bursts forth with:

> *"The Spirit of the Lord is upon me, because he hath anointed me to preach the gospel to the poor; he hath sent me to heal the broken hearted, to preach deliverance to the captives, and recovering of sight to the blind, to set at liberty them that are bruised, To preach the acceptable year of the Lord."*
>
> *Luke 4:18, 19*

The second revelation that Christ receives in the temptation concerns *mission*. He is urged by the devil to use His newfound power for personal gratification by turning stones to bread. The implication of this, in terms of leadership, is that it is a temptation to be popular. It is the temptation for relevancy. It is the temptation of "What do the people want?" rather than, "What do the people desperately need?" Jesus responds, *"...Man shall not live by bread alone, but by every word that proceedeth out of the mouth of God"* (Matthew 4:4).

Perhaps no two elements are more critical to spiritual formation than identity and mission. The two cohere and provide distinction between a "profession" and a "call." The effective fulfillment of "call" emerges out of what one is or has come to be. In true greatness, "being" always precedes doing. The outworking of call into effective leadership is not only the development of skills, but also is directly dependent upon the level of spiritual formation that takes place in the one being called. It is a mysterious merging of the internal self with divinity and divine purposes.

It should also be noted that there is no way to escape the conclusion that this process is genuinely transcendent. Certainly, such an encounter is not illogical. It is, however, "trans-logical." As Christ's ministry reveals, the results are nothing short of spectacular. But to attempt to describe such in a manner that is acceptable to sterile logic is impossible, even improper, and, perhaps, tantamount to desecration of a holy and sacred encounter. These events are spiritual beyond language. It is at once glorious but foreboding, revelatory but risky, enlightening but separating. These portals usher one into not only heavenly places, but also into places of the primal issues of life and death itself. While a thousand useful volumes speak of "Ten Steps" to this or "Twenty-One Principles" to that, the matters whereof we here speak issue from deeper waters. It is in the secret, the solemn, the ethereal, the lonely place. It is the haunt of demons. It is a place of angels. It is a place of wild beasts. It is a place near to life and death. It is the battlefield of spiritual struggle. It is the center, the place of God and the formation of spiritual dominion.

The third revelation of Christ's temptation focuses on *methods.* The first revelation is of *self-identity,* that is, understanding and accepting oneself from God's perspective.

(Is there another perspective?) The second revelation is one of *mission,* that is, the purpose of one's life from God's perspective. (Is there another authentic perspective?) The final revelation is one of *methods.*

Apparently pressed with the fear of rejection and the possible refusal of the people to accept His messiahship, Christ experiences the temptation to validate His call by something more than resting in the assurance of God's voice. The temptation is to create a dramatic public display of His power by leaping from the corner of the Temple wall and landing below unharmed. Instead, He responds by pointing out that God's methods do not need to be "proven" by experimental testing–that such attempts are, in fact, an act of unbelief and, therefore, sin.

Attempts to validate the Word of God by anything outside of the Word itself is a satanic temptation. The temptation to use God's power to "prove" one's leadership and gain respect is powerful. However, it is wrong to use any gifts, power, or knowledge to validate one's anointing in any way that does not fall within the perfect will of God for the specific mission assigned to the specific individual. Like Christ, a called person can have many gifts or abilities available that he may never appropriate for use in fulfilling God's specific will for his life. The tyranny of man is that one must "fulfill all of one's potential." But to God, a called person may be like a beautiful flower on the backside of an unnoticed hill. With exquisite beauty, which certainly qualifies for any king's table, it contentedly lives out its life unpicked and unseen, but fulfilling the purpose for which it was created, that is, to be beautiful to God. It is seen by God. It is valued by God. It is pleasing to God. That is enough. All other potential is placed on an altar and offered up to God in a fiery sacrifice. When this is done, God counts it as having been used to its fullest. This is not a waste of talent or charisma. This is placing it where it belongs—on the altar of sacrifice to God. Any other use is profane.

This particular point is of no little significance. Clearly, God often calls people to whom He has given a wide array of talents. Obedience to the call itself often further multiplies the gifts, or enablements, which makes one attractive and gifted above his/her worldly counterparts–a more powerful speaker, a more impacting singer or performer, etc. They may even be blessed with greater physical talents or beauty. Of course, these are things that are attractive to the world and temptation comes unbidden to use those gifts for unsacred purposes. These become distractions at the very least, and fatal pitfalls at worst. The call of God unequivocally makes all gifts and talents sacred and holy, set apart only for the use of God's service. This immediately disqualifies them for any use outside of holy pursuits and divine doings. God may use what He will and discard the rest. They are His. However, to use these enablements for any other purposes, including personal gain or glory to the flesh, is blasphemous and idolatrous. Scripture is certainly emphatic in this regard and the temptation for such is a very ancient trap.

It is also of major significance that Christ experiences all of this in the "wilderness." The wilderness is lonely, foreboding, and uncivilized. Like Moses and Elijah before him, Jesus becomes a man of the wilderness. This threesome has a universal bond forged and connected by the Spirit and the wilderness. Each, in turn, driven by the Spirit, finds a way through a wilderness with no roads and no direction markers. They "blaze" a trail by providing markers for all who will traverse this spiritual desert to life and leadership and dominion. Much later, it is Moses, Elijah, and Jesus who stand together on a mountain that transcends time, discussing Christ's passage through the ultimate, timeless, wilderness victory. We increasingly realize that the wilderness is a real place "in the spirit" in which deadly and desperate spiritual confrontation takes place and spiritual victories are won.

John the Baptist is also trained in the desert-wilderness, and he baptizes in the desert-wilderness. People interested in John's ministry must go to the wilderness to hear him. His ministry is a call to the wilderness. After His baptism, Jesus leaves the general areas of human habitation and journeys to this wilderness. Many other people also come to this wilderness. However, unlike the others, Jesus comes out of the waters of baptism and is driven deeper into this desert-wilderness. In this matter, the whole of His life is relentlessly telescoped and focused until the result is a complete distillation of His leadership potential and purpose. For Jesus, His call to be God's anointed is also a call to go to the wilderness and to return from the wilderness. What transpires at His baptism and in this wilderness is His defining moment and, without question, is the primary spiritual event instant of His life. Leadership on this level no longer allows one the luxury of an identity apart from God's mission. It is the ultimate relinquishing of rights and individual apart-ness.

While Matthew and Luke primarily refer to the desert as simply a geographic location, Mark, along with Old Testament writers, recognizes the special significance of the desert. Matthew and Luke focus on the elements of the temptation, but Mark focuses upon the fact that it occurs in the desert-wilderness. Some have assumed that Mark is simply less astute than the other two in recording the critical details of the event. Careful investigation reveals, however, that Mark does indeed know precisely what he is doing. A close reading of Mark 1:1-13 reveals that he is the only Gospel writer who recognizes that the desert-wilderness setting conveys its own fundamental theological message. Mark's repeated use of "desert" and "spirit" in these verses are clues frantically motioning to the reader to note something regarding the geographic location.

For Matthew and Luke, the temptation is about confrontation with the powers of evil. For Mark, the sole essential fact is that Jesus goes to the wilderness. It is the fact of the wilderness and His going there that is important. The desert itself must be recognized. Once this is understood, a window is opened to view a very broad, encompassing picture of not only what is transpiring during this forty days, but how this is a continuation of a fundamental and underlying theme embedded deep within, and deriving from, the Old Testament. In addition, it is a revelation of what will continue to be a basic characteristic of the remainder of Christ's ministry, for He repeatedly returns alone to the desert-wilderness throughout His ministry.

As we have seen, the three Gospel accounts of Christ's baptism and temptation reveal a struggle of the interior life at the deepest level. The outworking of this struggle eventually penetrates every crevice and crease, not only in His life, but in the entire universe. The sweep and scope of such potential is cradled within a single, called individual! The struggle is no fantasy, no delusion of the overworked mind, but rather, is genuine and great. The potential result is equally great.

The story of the Old Testament must be understood within the context of this relationship to the desert. In both Testaments, the desert is filled with temptation, with trial, with fiery serpents, and with wild beasts. The development of God's son, Israel, takes place in the wilderness. Sinai, the place of formation of Israel's identity as a nation, is in the wilderness. There they wander, but their wandering is not aimless. God has a goal for their development. God has led them into the wilderness and only He can bring them out. Israel makes an attempt to shorten the time of waiting, seeking to escape the desert before God allows them to do so. The result is devastating (Mauser, 1963).

Repeatedly identified as God's "son," Israel, upon being "called out," must then journey through the wilderness and overcome it. Equally emphatic, Jesus as God's Son, also being "called," is driven straight into the wilderness for development, for self-identity, and for spiritual formation (Mark 1:12). He is the new Israel. What the first Israel could not accomplish corporately, He accomplishes individually. The journey into the wilderness must precede public ministry and power. Only after this purgation of the soul does great ministry and leadership come to pass.

The notion of blessing in the Old Testament is consistently connected with this idea of obtaining the land, a land which is tamed and fruitful. Inhabited and cultivated by God's people, it is a place of safety, rest, and productivity. But, as we have seen, the wilderness is diametrical to all of the above. Desert lands are cursed lands bereft of water, cultivation, and normal life. They are the home of undesirable and frightening beings. Fiery and venomous serpents, predatory fowl, carrion eaters, porcupines, hyenas, jackals, and other wild beasts dwell there. It is home to wild asses, vultures, and hedgehogs (Isaiah 32:14, Zephaniah 2: 14, Ezekiel 34:5, 25). All of this has spiritual connotations, as reinforced by references to the satyr and the hag (Numbers 21:6-9, Deuteronomy 8:15, Isaiah 34:9-15). In contrast, neither cattle, nor other domesticated animals, nor birds are found there (Jeremiah 9:10). Further, good land can become desert in which, as a consequence of sin, productivity and pleasantness are lost and the land reverts to a pre-cultivated haunt of barrenness and demonic spirits (Jeremiah 12:4, 49: 18, 50:40). Thus, any place abandoned by God is likened to wilderness. It is a broken-down, decaying place where the population and progress have been lost. Roads and direction have been destroyed and cities lie in silent ruin in mute testimony to judgment.

It is Christ Himself who connects this notion of spiritual wasteland to the human soul. When cleansed, the soul is likened to a house out of which evil spirits are cast. However, when the house is left unfilled (i.e., by the Holy Spirit), these spirits are described as going into a "desert place." This place is obviously the haunt and habitation of other spirits that wander there. The displaced spirit recruits even more spirits out of this barren wasteland like, or worse than, himself and returns to the house from which he has been driven. Finding the house empty, he re-inhabits it, along with the seven additional spirits he has brought with him. These homeless, vagabond spirits obviously seek reentry into inhabited areas. Here in the desert, then, is the place where dominion over such spirits is gained.

Christ goes deep into the desert-wilderness, as does John the Baptist, Israel, Moses, and Elijah. All experience formation there. It is a place elevated beyond petty turf wars, competition and rivalry. Can one who has not experienced this lonely journey into vicious hostility truly understand the value of intimacy, love, friendship, brotherhood, and community? Can it be that, in doing everything possible to avoid the painful confrontation with raw human loneliness that accompanies such an encounter, we allow ourselves to become imprisoned by deceitful gods with shallow remedies and assurances of relief? The almost visceral tendency to pull back from this harsh, elemental confrontation seems to be the one battle that must be won if a leader is to experience high-level spiritual leadership. Loneliness cannot be removed from the experience. One stands alone. One experiences alone. "No love, friendship, intimate embrace, tender kiss, no community, commune, or collective, no man or woman, will ever be able to satisfy our desire to be released from our lonely condition," declares Henri Nouwen (1972). Spiritual "greats" are driven into this parched and cursed place where, in some sense beyond present understanding, cities once flourished but are now left unattended and in shambles, the inhabitants having been driven out by judgment. Only scorched and barren land remains.

"Upon the land of my people shall come up thorns and briers; yea, upon all the houses of joy in the joyous city: Because the palaces shall be forsaken; the multitude of the city shall be left; the forts and towers shall be for dens for ever, a joy of wild asses, a pasture of flocks..."
Isaiah 32: 13, 14

By now, some may be wondering whether such a journey is for them. The answer is, maybe not. Also, there are probably degrees to which various people penetrate into these areas of formation and this may well be as it should. However, for Jesus, there are no degrees of penetration into such high places. He goes all the way. He conquers all and, as a servant, fulfills all the potential that God holds for Him. Thus, to follow Him is to utterly relinquish control of one's life. It is to surrender unequivocally to Him and His will. To follow Him includes journeying to the barren place where walls have fallen, where cities lie in ruins, and where strange and ugly heads are raised to thwart renewal.

Lucifer himself is declared to be the cause of this wilderness that resulted from rebellion. Pride is sin. Sin brings destruction and desolation. Thus, Lucifer is responsible for "destroying cities" and being the one who makes *the world a wilderness*" (Isaiah 14:17). The prophecy is that he is "cut down to the ground," and the prophet declares with no small wonder, "How art thou fallen from heaven, O Lucifer..." (Isaiah 14:12). The land once inhabited and filled with nobles (i.e., government, social order, culture, etc.) is gone. Now,

"They shall call the nobles...but none shall be there...And thorns shall come up in her palaces, nettles and brambles in the fortresses thereof: and it shall be an habitation of dragons, and a court for owls."
Isaiah 34:12, 13

The Hebrew word translated as "dragons" refers to unknown, wailing creatures of the night, the place of nocturnal beasts, the habitation of owls. It is a forsaken place with whispering winds mourning over the broken remains of yesterday's hopes. Interestingly, when Christ is driven into the wilderness, the only life forms mentioned there are God, Satan, Jesus the man, wild beasts, and angels. What are these wild beasts? Are they real beasts or some other kind of beasts?

> *"The wild beasts of the desert shall also meet with the wild beasts of the island, and the satyr shall cry to his fellow; the screech owl also shall rest there, and find for herself a place of rest. There shall the great owl make her nest, and lay, and hatch, and gather under her shadow: there shall the vultures also be gathered, every one with her mate."*   Isaiah 34:14, 15

The "hag" and the "satyr" are found in the desert. The most apt description of these is that they are thought to be demons in animal form. A satyr is identified as a wandering demonic creature lurking somewhere between beast and human. Greek mythology defines it as a minor deity of the woods attendant upon Bacchus, the god of lechery, drunkenness, and lustfulness. A satyr is described as having pointed ears and shaggy hair, a cross between a goat and a man (the goat, of course, exemplifying a variety of demonic activities and symbols). Even today, the term "satyriasis" describes the abnormal condition of a man who has an uncontrollable desire for sexual intercourse. Thus, the wilderness is the haunt of the nether world, the demonic, the lost, the directionless, the addicted.

The reader may, at this point, wonder if we have not strayed from the original concept of spiritual formation taking place in the deep rather than in the desert. These two places seem like opposites: wet versus arid, fluidity versus fixity, etc. However, Mark provides the startling revelation that the wilderness realm is closely tied to the realms of the deep and of death, and all three of these realms comprise the shadowy, invisible world (Ezekiel 26:19-21). The element common to all of them is chaos, the condition where the curse prevails (Mauser, 1963). The condition that is starkly outlined in Genesis 1:2 can clearly be seen as the motif of judgment, disaster, darkness, and chaos. The wilderness is a place akin to the deep of the sea. Both are metaphors for places of profound, life-altering spiritual battle and development. While the sea emphasizes the fluidity of such places, the desert, or wilderness, emphasizes dreariness, barrenness, and hostility to any life other than feral, untamed things.

In Mark, the wilderness and the mountain are also often closely connected and used similarly. The mountain is consistently marked as a place of repeated retreat (cp. Mark 3:13; 6:46) and the setting for stupendous revelatory events (e.g., 9:2, 13:3). Jesus goes into the wilderness to be tempted, but it is a mountain—a mountain in and part of the wilderness. Like the desert, the mountain is referenced not simply as a geographic location, but as a metaphor heavily weighted with theological content. Sheol, death, and the waters of the sea are utilized repeatedly to describe the trauma experienced by those called to lead. Surrounded by malevolent forces, those who go there are set upon by all of the dark and sinister powers of the netherworld that attempt to utterly thwart them and their ministry. It is a chaos from which God's servants, tossed in turmoil, cry for help and He rescues them (Psalm 18:7-19). It is a place of monsters and dragons. The Psalmist declares:

> *"Thou didst divide the sea by thy strength; thou brakest the heads of the dragons in the waters. Thou brakest the heads of leviathan in pieces, and gavest him to be meat to the people inhabiting the wilderness. Thou didst cleave the fountain and the flood: thou driedst up mighty rivers."*
> *Psalm 74:13-15*

This battle is with leviathan, the multi-headed dragon of chaos. God is seen as *"the God that doeth wonders,"* and the psalmist declares, *"Thy way is in the sea, and thy path in the great waters, and thy footsteps are not known"* (Psalm 77:14, 19). Both the psalmist and Saint Mark equate leviathan and wild beasts to Satan.

The foreboding nature of the desert causes disciples, both then and now, to resist direct contact with the evil forces therein. As a place of attack and confrontation, the desert is no place for the neophyte who grasps neither the nature of the desert nor its implications. Such understandings derive from encountering that which they have not yet encountered. **The disciples' lives lack the imprint that their Master's life possesses, an imprint that results only from frontal encounter with the desert and its powers. In contrast to them, Christ experiences a "defining moment," a primary spiritual event instant in which He comes face-to-face with His own destiny in the spirit-world of confrontation and battle with the forces of darkness.** His entrance is neither gradual nor progressive. There is a "specific instant" at which time He is ushered away from everyday life and catapulted into the arena of the great, the mighty, the terrible. Here, deep in the Spirit, He peers off the edge of surface existence into the vast world of spiritual realities and possibilities. It is extreme. It is radical to the extent that His life is fundamentally and radically altered from that point on. He can never be the same. There is no going back. Seeing what He sees alters Him. Past understandings are revised. Present lifestyle undergoes violent change. Future plans suffer fundamental revision. The changes are severe and the demands are radical. However, accompanying revelation of the breadth and depth of the conflict is also revelation of the cosmic, universal nature of the victory. This vision carries Christ to the place of complete triumph. He now sees the fierce opposing forces from the finish rather than from the perspective of the present struggle. His secret is that henceforth He will view the conflict from the ultimate back to the penultimate, rather than looking forward through a fog of doubt toward an uncertain future. For Him, the future is already. "It is finished." He will not be extrapolating out of the present situation the methods for future victory. Rather, He will see Himself as bringing the finished future back into the present. Therefore, each miracle, each spiritual victory, each testament to a life changed, is simply a "sign" that the future is, indeed, completed by Christ, of which these are evidences, brought backward into the present as ongoing testimonies to Christ's victory. Every "Son of God" experiences this process of formation.

Sons of God

It is interesting that scripture reserves the term "son" or "sons of God" exclusively for those who are "sons" by special creation and never by natural birth. For example, angels are termed "sons of God" and are, of course, not born, but of special creation. Likewise, Adam is also called "son of God." Though fully human, he was of special creation and not of natural birth. In similar fashion, as a nation, Israel is also called God's son. In the record of nations, only Israel is of special creation by God Himself and God alone. Then, Jesus is the Son of God by special creation in the womb of a virgin (Luke 1:35). Finally, those "born from above" (John 3:3,5) of the Spirit are the sons of God, *"born not of blood, nor of the will of the flesh, nor of the will of man, but of God"* (John 1:13).

All of the above who are termed "sons of God" are deeply intertwined with the history of earth, indeed of the entire universe. This issue of primacy in the earth is the main issue in the temptation of Jesus. These issues are so primal, so rudimentary, and so seminal that they go straight to the very nadir of all that has to do with earth.[1] This struggle goes

---

[1] It is interesting to note that the environmental and ecological well-being of the earth itself is, in scripture, repeatedly connected to the moral and spiritual issues of mankind. Such is the case with the fall of Adam, the flood of Noah, the land of Israel and the eventual time of the New Heaven and New Earth.

far back into antiquity, far beyond the history of man. It is a struggle not only for man's emancipation but for earth's emancipation—for the emancipation of the universe itself. There is nothing like this elsewhere in human history. All other heroics of the nations pale pitifully in the light of this triumph. Christ alone stands victorious on the "exceeding high mountain" from which can be viewed the earth, the cosmos, and the history of all of the empires and the glory of them. This means the stakes in leadership ministry are staggering. We have entered into an enterprise so weighty that the only worthy responses are awe, wonder, and reverence. May God help us to realize this.

Unfortunately, there is a paucity of information from either religious or secular sources that gives us a clear picture of earth's history. Archaeology and geology provide sparse information. However, some believe there are occasional small windows in scripture through which brief glimpses of the antiquity of this history can possibly be seen. These, combined with minimal logic, may provide helpful insights. Some of these are as follows:

- Isaiah 45:18 clearly states that the creation of earth was orderly and that it was to be inhabited—nothing like the chaos we find in Genesis 1:2.
- Chapter 28 of Ezekiel contains a prophecy to the King of Tyre. Reading it reveals that it is a prophecy with both a local fulfillment as well as a wider ranging application (which is not unusual in prophecy). In this case, it is Lucifer himself and the account of his fall. Included in this account is the declaration *"Thou hast been in Eden the Garden of God..."* (v. 13). The remainder of the passage seems to clearly indicate that the time spoken of precedes Adam and Eve.
- This prophecy, when combined with statements found in Isaiah 14:9-17, may well indicate that Lucifer had dominion on earth prior to the creation of Adam, but

lost it with his rebellion, thus becoming the one *"that made the world as a wilderness..."* (v.17). Additional scriptures such as Ezekiel 26:19 state: *"For thus saith the Lord God; when I shall make thee a desolate city, like the cities that are not inhabited when I shall bring up the deep upon thee, and great waters shall cover thee."*

This prophecy may also apply to Lucifer and his fall. And is this scripture perhaps also a description of how the earth became "without form and void" as we find it in Genesis 1:2? Some believe Jeremiah 4:23-28 is also an anointed utterance that pulls back the curtain on a judgement so crushing that the earth itself is plunged into blackness and a deep freeze. What all may Jeremiah be referencing when he declares:

"I beheld the earth, and, lo, it was without form, and void; and the heavens, and they had no light. I beheld the mountains, and, lo, they trembled, and all the hills moved lightly. I beheld, and, lo, there was no man, and all the birds of the heavens were fled. I beheld, and lo, the fruitful place was a wilderness, and all the cities thereof were broken down at the presence of the Lord, and by His fierce anger. For this hath the Lord said, the whole land shall be desolate; yet will I not make a full end. For this shall the earth mourn and the heavens above be black; because I have spoken it, I have purposed it, and will not repent, neither will I turn back from it."   *Jeremiah 4:23-28*

In spite of the limited information about the earth's history, there can be little question that it is a special place. In a universe in which we now know there are trillions of stars and billions of galaxies, with distances and speeds beyond comprehension (a dust cloud was recently observed on Jupiter 3 million miles high), we also now know that the universe is rapidly expanding! Where is it going? We do not know. What we do know is that in these trillions of heavenly bodies, not a *single one has been found to have life on it— not one—except earth*. And such tenuous life! If the energy of creation force were different by one part in 1,000,000,0 00,000,000,000,000,000,000,000,000,000,000,000,000,00 0,000,000,000,000,000,000,000,000,000,000,000,000,000, 000,000,000,000,000,000,000,000,000, then life as we know it would cease to exist. That is, if that energy were adjusted by just one part out of this unthinkable number, all would die (Schroeder, 1997). That earth holds a position of primacy in the universe as we know it, there can be no doubt. It is this earth, this universe, this cosmos, of which Satan says to Christ, "all these things will I give thee, if thou wilt fall down and worship me." Is it possible to comprehend the scope of what was connected with, and was compressed into, this one temptation? All of space, all of history, all of time, is being negotiated. Is it possible to comprehend the far-reaching effects of Christ's confrontation here? Out of this victory emerges His ministry, and consequently, our ministry (John 17:18). The breadth and depth and universality of such a ministry is of staggering proportions: may God help us to enter it with appropriate sobriety.

Son of God, Jesus
vs.
son of God, Lucifer

As an angel, Lucifer is recorded in the book of Job as coming to God along with the other "sons of God," which are obviously angelic. Lucifer is also termed *"son of the morning"* (Isaiah 14:12). Thus, the confrontation at Christ's temptation is between the former "son of the morning" who has lost his preeminence but regained power on earth through the fall of Adam, and Christ, the Son of God who has come to not only wrest man and earth from Satan's control, but to effect the deliverance of the entire creation from the consequences of sin and judgment (Romans 8:22, 23). In terms of the man Christ Jesus, this is a battle between two "strong men" in which Satan controls the house and its contents but in which Christ breaks in and violently defeats the inhabitant, disarming him, thrusting him out, taking the contents and dividing the spoils (Matthew 12:29).

Usually the New Testament tone is one of measured statements when addressing issues such as taunting or exulting over one's enemies. In this case, this is not so. Colossians 2:15 boldly declares that Christ defeats Satan and makes an "open show" of him. Other translations state that Christ holds him up to "public exhibition" and "open contempt." Using the imagery of a Roman general returning from a triumphal conquest of a foreign land, the reader of this passage knows full well what it means. Such generals, upon return to Rome, conduct a parade down the main thorough-fares with the vanquished king in tow, in utter humiliation and contempt. Such is the complete, resounding, and public victory of the Son of God over the son of the morning.

Son of God, Jesus
vs.
Son of God, Adam

There are striking similarities between the temptation of Adam and Eve and the temptation of Christ. Both arise from temptation regarding eating, regarding implicit obedience, and regarding the lust of the flesh and the pride of life. Both also revolve around selfishness, the temptation to take short-cuts, and the temptation to seek outside validation of God's Word apart from trust in the Word as being self-authenticating.

The results of the fall of Adam resonate far beyond Adam. Adam and Eve fall under judgment and the earth falls under judgment. In addition, the whole human race falls under judgment. Man is expelled from the Garden, severing his daily communion with God. An angel with a flaming sword is placed at the entrance to the Garden, denying access to the Tree of Life and to union with God. Any who would enter are cut down without mercy and without fail.

It is a remarkable thing that for thousands of years billions of humans have died and none have ever returned. Not ten. Not five. Not even one. Many ingenious people have lived but no one has found a cure for death. One should not suppose that men have not tried. History is filled with bizarre attempts to triumph over death. These range from placing food in the tombs of ancient pharaohs to modern cryonics (freezing the dead body in hopes of someday finding a way to revive it—maybe with someone else's head, etc.) or cryobiosis (i.e., freezing the body shortly before death).

Other attempts have centered around spiritism. For example, the famous magician Harry Houdini (1874-1926) made an agreement with his wife before he died that the first of the two of them to die was to try to communicate with the survivor. He devised a ten-word code that he would communicate to his wife, if possible, within ten years after his death. After he died, various mediums claimed that they were able to establish contact with him, but none was able to transmit to his wife the predetermined code. His widow declared the experiment a failure before her death in 1943.

More recently, the New Age Movement has attempted connection beyond death by channeling and contacting "spirit guides." The best known attempts are through propagation of the doctrine of reincarnation (i.e., the teaching that we all lived previously in some other "life form" and have "progressed" through form after form to where we are today). The idea is both very old and very unbiblical and is simply another attempt to alleviate the finality of death. Socrates massaged this idea with the dualistic notion that the soul/mind functions better when detached from the body; therefore, death is to be desired (of course, Socrates expounded this idea, according to Phaedo, on the day of his execution). This fallacious idea persisted throughout the 400 years from the time of the Greeks until the time of Christ. It even crept into the early church and had to be expunged (Colossians 2:20-23). In contrast, the Bible teaches that freedom does not come from death and dissolution of the body, but rather, from life and transformation of the body.

All of the above ideas are attempts to regain entrance to the Garden and access to the Tree of Life, which the first Adam lost. The challenge is to defeat or circumvent the Cherubim (angel) with the whirling sword that cuts down all who would enter. This includes every great human scientist, philanthropist, military leader and all of the renowned explorers, such as Ponce de Leon, who sought for the fountain of youth and life. All failed.

It is the victory of Christ over death in resurrection, which has, for the first time, breached this previously impenetrable wall. Jesus is thus called the "archegon," or "captain," "trailbazer," or "pioneer" of the human race. He "blasts" (John 1) the darkness and provides light for those who have sat in darkness since Adam. This is the good news!

"For since by man came death, by man came also the resurrection of the dead."   1 Corinthians 15:21

The history of humanity is one long, unending graveyard stretching from Eden to Calvary. Even now, men continue to lead assault on the Cherubim with the flaming sword in futile attempts to regain entrance to the Garden. The stack of skulls outside the Garden, wherein is the Tree of Life, has grown through the centuries. Included are the bones of the ages and of famous men and women. Herculean efforts are represented by the chalky pile whose silence is born on the wind across the landscape of history with the tearful lament, "We have failed." All great human conquests lie broken at the defending angel's feet. Given thousands of years to use their wisdom to defeat the sword, man's ingenuity and wisdom fails. Tired, sighing, and exhausted, the world lies in darkness and failure.

The seers of the Old Testament, however, look far off into the distance and see One who catches their attention. Because He is powerful, they dub Him "the Lion of the Tribe of Judah" (Genesis 49:9, Revelation 5:5). Through the mist of history, they peer intently into the distance and excitedly query:

"Who is this who cometh from Edom, with dyed garments from Bozrah? This that is glorious in his apparel, travelling in the greatness of his strength?"
Isaiah 63:1

Through the telescope of prophetic revelation, they watch this One make His way closer to the swinging sword of the vigilant Cherubim. Coming ever closer through the swirling mist of history, everything in proximity to the Garden tingles with expectation. The atmosphere crackles with a resolute determination to break through to the tree beyond the sword. The last Adam passes by the centuries of decayed human efforts which lie in a silent heap of failed hopes. Then, as no other has ever done, the "second man" Christ does not attempt to attack the angel, but rather, comes to a point just beyond the sword where He opens a scroll which He holds in his hands. John, in Revelation 5, representing the whole human race, weeps (verse 2) because no man has been legally qualified to take back the scroll of the legal title to earth, which includes the Garden of Eden and all that is therein. Paul declares the whole creation groaning and travailing together in pain...waiting for redemption (Romans 8). The angel, ready to defend against all comers, inspects the scroll. When he realizes that the scroll is the legal title deed to the earth, it begins to dawn on him that the One who stands before him is not just another would-be challenger trying to enter the Garden. This One can not only enter the Garden, he owns it! Further shock registers on the face of the angel as he recognizes the conqueror to also be his Creator. The authority to stop the pendulum swing of the sword which has swung for thousands of years has finally arrived. For the first time since there were only two people on the earth, the Cherubim steps aside, and bows, declaring, "Enter, Oh Worthy One!" Turning, with a voice like the sound of a trumpet, the shout is made. "He has prevailed to open the book" (Revelation 5:7-9). The sword stops! The whirling sound of its movement has been, for thousands of years, the background noise of the universe. But now, angels and humans become aware of the new quietness. Suddenly, the sound of failure and of rejection is silenced. In the distance, what can only be described as the sound of many voices can be heard, the number of which is "ten thousand times ten thousand and thousands of thousands" (Revelation 5:11). They are shouting with all their combined might to Him who stands victorious on the horizon of the universe:

> *"Worthy is the Lamb that was slain to receive power, and riches, and wisdom, and strength, and honour, and glory, and blessing. Blessing and honour, and glory, and power be unto him...[even] unto the Lamb forever and ever."* Revelation 5:12-14

Though the above description utilizes a little literary license, nevertheless, such is the victory of Christ, the Son of God, in redeeming the failure of Adam, the Son of God.

Jesus, the Individual Son of God
vs.
Israel, the Corporate Son of God

We have looked rather closely at the temptation of Christ as recorded in Matthew, Mark, and Luke. Both Mark and Luke focus on particularities with which they are impressed. It is Matthew, however, with insight and ability equal to that of any biblical writer, who best preserves the content and does so with extremely pure and penetrating construction. Once one grasps the scope that Matthew includes in his account, it becomes evident that this is not written by a simple mind with a passing acquaintance with Christ. Striking complexity lies beneath its surface simplicity and pauciloquence. Matthew utilizes every communication device he can to broaden the application of the story. One cannot recognize the variety of thought connections by simply studying the few verses of the confrontation. It is overtly connected to Deuteronomy chapters 6-8, but also extends deep into the entirety of Deuteronomy and the Exodus from Egypt. Jesus fulfills what Israel failed.

That Israel is also God's Son is made very clear. Besides the clear scriptural statements (Exodus 4:22, Jeremiah 31:9, Hosea 11:1, Deuteronomy 1:31, 8:5), there are numerous other obvious representations of Israel as the Son of God in the desert wanderings. In Christ's temptation, the "Son of God" thought is primary to the whole of it. Next to this, in terms of primacy, is the idea of temptation. Both of these ideas tie directly to God's dealing with Israel as a Son in the wilderness.

> *"And thou shalt remember all the way which the Lord thy God led thee these forty years in the wilderness, to humble thee, and to prove thee, to know what was in thine heart, whether thou wouldest keep his commandments, or no. Thou shalt also*

consider in thine heart, that, as a man chasteneth
his son, so the Lord thy God chasteneth thee."
Deuteronomy 8:2, 5

As should be clear by now, the idea of temptation is meant as a testing of a covenant relationship to ascertain if the partner will keep his side of the agreement. God never tests the ungodly and the heathen, but only those who are His own. God's side is to fulfill all responsibilities of the covenant that pertain to Him as God—to be in their midst, to be their God—and to give divine blessing as promised (i.e., life, health, food, protection, provision, and triumph over enemies). In turn, the person/people in covenant are to be faithful, obedient, and careful to keep their ministry limited to pleasing the Father alone. Numerous ancient rabbis have noted a double meaning in verses regarding temptation, which applies directly to leadership formation. They contend that temptation not only disciplines, but prepares for future promotion and recognition. Thus, we once again see why this primary spiritual event instant becomes the defining moment of one's ministry for the remainder of one's life.

The parallels between Christ's temptation as the Son of God and Israel's temptation as the Son of God in the wilderness are unmistakable. Some of these links are as follows:

- Christ's forty days correspond to Israel's 40 years. Moses is also on the mount for forty days. That 40 days and 40 years can be corresponding periods can be seen in Numbers 14:34, where 40 years of punishment are earned for 40 days of grumbling while spying out the land (cp. Ezekiel 4:5).
- The temptation for Moses deals with bread for the corporate Son, that is, Israel. The temptation of Jesus compresses the authority of those corporate hopes, promises, and failures into individual confrontation again, over bread. Like Adam and Eve, the temptation is

connected to desire, to craving. Israel is also tempted with the same, leading to Kibroth-Hattavah, that is *"graves of craving"* (Numbers 11:34).

> *"And they tempted God in their heart by asking meat for their lust."* Psalm 78:18

Whereas Israel opts for the "prove it first" life, Jesus opts for the "faith-life," a life which, on the surface, often appears undesirable and uncertain. It requires trusting God's Word in the face of seemingly contradictory circumstances. It requires surrender of one's control of self into the will of the Father and then accepting the results, whether or not they are what was expected. To be dissatisfied with the faith-life means that "you have rejected Jehovah who is among you" (Numbers 11:20, Psalm 78:22; 106). The faith-life demands waiting on God. Those who do so, such as Jesus, experience "angels ministering to him." What did those angels minister? Were they not bringing him bread? Dinner with angels as waiters is available only to those of the faith-life. This arena of exclusive service is, indeed, for the few. It is a rarefied atmosphere that many simply never know or find.

Christ's victory over hunger lust represents victory in the wilderness—a victory Israel did not attain—which certifies God's protection in the wilderness. In turn, Christ's victory in the temple represents God's protection in hallowed places. The battle is now removed from the wilderness to the central place of divine activity, from the howling place to the holy place. One constant in Jewish literature is that the temple represents a place of safety and protection. The Psalms contain a whole section that reinforces this idea (48:3, 57:2, 61:5, 63:8). This is a temptation on the pinnacle or "wing" of the temple. The temptation is to seek a sign, through experimentation, which will authenticate God's promises. But the covenant Son cannot demand a sign other than to trust the already established Word, for to do so is not consistent with the faith-life. The temple "wing" or pinnacle, the place of execution for those to be thrown down or stoned, is a challenge to Jesus to test the faithfulness of God's Word.

Finally, Jesus is taken to a "high mountain" where He can behold the kingdoms of the world and the glory of them. This is not beholding with only the physical eye. The stakes are incredibly high. It is a cosmic negotiation for real estate and all that is on it, including man.

In these negotiations, Satan is following an ancient legal custom. When one is attempting to convey property to another, the seller takes the buyer to some vantage point. Here the buyer assures the seller of his desire to transfer the property, and allows the buyer to see it—to receive it with his own eyes. We are not speaking here, then, of a mere transfer of power. We are speaking of lavish glories which were typical of Eastern kings. Satan is acting as a good salesman and a good lawyer (Daube, 1947). Whereas God handed over the promised land to the leader of Israel, Satan here attempts to do the same to Christ and with the same requirements, that is, to worship the one doing the transfer. This is a loyalty test. Who will you "sign-up" with—the yet unanswered Word of promise that is of the faith-life or the seemingly instant gratification of a short-cut to the glory and success for which you have come?

The above temptation reveals how complex the decisions one makes can become. For example, a leader can labor for years without success in seeing one's ministrerial dreams come to pass. In the meantime, some find success, but with a price. Their success requires compromises, or simply remaining silent in areas in which the message conflicts with present lifestyles. They may have become famous. Doors open for their ministry, their books, their products, etc. They receive notoriety and glory. It looks like the blessings of God. Others, seeing this, are mightily tempted to follow, and many do so. However, one must consider what they are required to bow to in order to gain this "success." The hunger of Christ's body for bread is no more tempting than His hunger for success in that mission for which God has sent Him. We can be quite certain that Matthew does not include all that was said, nor does he record how long this mountain meeting lasts. It seems probable that Satan uses every seductive enticement in his arsenal to bring Christ under his dominion. No temptation is perhaps more powerful, more tempting, than to acquiesce to that which is unclean in order to reach the desired goals. Nevertheless, opportunity for success, however gently wrapped in compromises of core values, is not success, but capitulation and defeat. The road to compromise can look so sweet, but always companies with deception and falsehood. As a new wave of such seeming success begins to crest, wise men say, "I believe I will sit this one out."

It is not an accident that all three of Christ's responses to Satan's temptations are found in the book of Deuteronomy. Further, it is no accident that all three (Deuteronomy 8:3, 6:16, 10:20) are found after the Shema in Deuteronomy 6:5 which states:

> *"And thou shalt love the Lord thy God with all thine heart, and with all thy soul, and with all thy might."*

This is the greatest of all commandments for God's sons, whether Adam, or Israel, or Christ. It is the one commandment in which God must try His "covenant partner" and must know whether the son's loyalty matches the covenant. The temptations of Adam, of Israel, and of Christ revolve around the question of whether they can affirm that they are obedient to Deuteronomy 6:5. It is the minimum requirement because, for God's leader to carry out the mission, God must place enormous power and authority in his hands—authority, power, and trust which will not be breached in the time of extreme temptation to do so. In this, Adam fails. Israel also fails. But Christ succeeds. "Succeeds in what?" one may ask. He succeeds in loving the Lord so much, that is, with all His heart, with all His soul, and with all His might, that He does not waver when faced with ingenious contrivances designed to seduce Him to do otherwise.

First, to love God with the "whole heart" references one's inclinations, strong desires, cravings, lusts. Israel in the wilderness is filled with "strong cravings," as is Adam. They both fail the "love the Lord thy God with all thy heart" test. In contrast, Jesus, in His role as Messiah, refuses to allow cravings to supplant His love for God with all His heart.

Next, to love God with the "whole soul" ("life") is to choose pleasing God and being loyal to His revealed will over life itself. Here the soul is equal to one's life. His will is greater than His life. God's will is life itself. Satan tempts Christ to access the Father's protection of His life by forcing God to do so. But for those who love God with all their soul-life, their love is not needful of security outside of the Father's Word, for it alone is enough. We must minister based on His Word alone, needing no proof of its reliability before proceeding. Divine order does not have "Word" following "signs," but rather signs following the Word.

Finally, to love God with one's whole might, according to the rabbis, is to love Him with one's whole property. One's property is their "might." Thus, Jesus is tempted to love the gaining of the "property" or kingdoms, which His ministry is ordained to win, more than He loves the God for whom He is winning it. This is, indeed, a sophisticated temptation in which the temptation is to gain precisely what the Father has ordained He should gain, that is, the world and all its kingdoms. Hence, what is revealed here is that one may actually attain the goals given by God, but do so in ways that are unacceptable to the Father. God does not need "Egyptian alliances or Assyrian horses." His people are, first and foremost, a walking obedient people.

It is especially interesting that not only does Satan offer Jesus the kingdoms, but also the glory of them (Matthew 4:8). God's will for Him carries with it the temptation of reaching objectives in a way in which the promised glory can be gained through disobedience. Again, it is impossible for us to grasp the enormity of this victory. Plunging backward into the mist of the far-distant past, Christ's victory removes every cursed result of the failures of Lucifer the Son, Adam the Son, and Israel the Son. Going the other direction, that is, forward, Christ's victory, with lightning speed, travels to the end and finishes the work of redemption. The end result of Christ's faithfulness in fulfilling Deuteronomy 6:5 is found in 1 Corinthians 15:28. Here Christ does something Satan, and all leaders like him, will never do.

"And when all things shall be subdued unto him, then shall the Son also himself be subject unto him that put all things under him, that God may be all in all."
1 Corinthians 15:28

This is not a description of one God-person being subject to another. No, this is about God's human Son, God's leader, God's perfect minister, bringing the fruit of His ministry— both its methods and its results—and laying them at the feet of Him to whom all belongs, that is, to the Father, to God who is Lord of all. Christ thus never thinks of His ministry as being His. Nor does He take His ministerial success as His own. His leadership gifts belong to the Father. His victories belong to the Father. His personal being belongs to the Father. His total obedience to both means and ends belongs to the Father. He knows they cannot be separated. To use illicit means is to arrive at illicit ends. This is what it means to love the Lord thy God with all thy heart, with all thy soul, and with all thy might. Results are not enough. Methods matter. Character matters. Process matters. Product that derives from tainted processes won't do. Casting out devils is not enough. One must know and obey the Father. True ministry is ministry only unto the Father.

The temptation to "short-cut" is given to Jesus as an alternative to the plan given Him by God. "Bow down to me," He is encouraged, and "I will give you the kingdoms of the world." No cross, no rejection, no struggle. Satan is correct that the battle is for dominion over the earth. But the methods for attaining this must be God's. The purposes of Christ are far-reaching, and through Him the entirety of the cosmos will be "redeemed" (Colossians 1:20, 21).

The mistaken logic behind this temptation is that "means" are not important, rather, only "ends." In the things of God, however, means and ends are intertwined. In many ways, means and ends are one. Using means other than God's often aborts the desired ends. There is a vital relationship between mission and method. In divine work, methods not only lead to completion of mission, but are themselves part of mission.

We conclude that, in His capacity as the Son of God, Jesus overcomes every failure of every earlier personage or group so-called. Lucifer manifests rebellion and unbelief, but Christ manifests faith and obedience. Adam manifests rebellion and unbelief, but Christ manifests faith and obedience. Israel manifests rebellion and unbelief, but Christ manifests faith and obedience. Lucifer experiences success in temporarily gaining the kingdoms of the world and the glory of them, but fails the obedience test. His ministry is not a ministry unto the Father, but unto self. Adam sees personal gratification, self-improvement, and self-advancement outside of God's will for his life, and fails the obedience test. His is not a ministry unto only the Father. Likewise, there is Israel, represented by Moses...can our heart but weep when we ponder Moses?

Moses has led Israel to the Promised Land but he cannot go in. Why? Because he fails the obedience test by striking the rock. Little did he know the far-reaching symbolism that one act of a divinely-called leader can carry. Other than Christ, there has never been a leader, secular or religious, like Moses. He is the most complete leader in history. Nevertheless, after 40 years of wilderness leadership, he cannot go into the Promised Land. In this, he represents Israel, who never enters God's spiritual land of rest (see Hebrews 4:7-11, 8:9-13). Even so, there is no scene in the Old Testament more touching than the final days of Moses. God and Moses are like two old friends—like a father and a grown son—possessing a depth of mutual love and intimacy beyond words. He is God's man, God's leader. Moses asks if he can enter the Promised Land. God, with sadness, explains that he cannot do that, but then slowly walks together with him from the plains to the top of a high mountain. Here he is allowed to view the present kingdoms of the world and the glory of them. They stand together in silence admiring the land:

> *"And the Lord showed him all the land of Gilead, unto Dan, And all Naphtali, and the land of Ephraim, and Manasseh, and all the land of Judah, unto the utmost sea, And the south, and the plain of the valley of Jericho, the city of palm trees, unto Zoar. And the Lord said unto him, This is the land..."*
> *Deuteronomy 34:1-4*

One can hardly read this, and then read of Jesus upon a high mountain to view the kingdoms over which He seeks conquest, and fail to make some connection—especially when the whole temptation response of Jesus is also taken entirely out of the Book of Deuteronomy.

So Moses dies having failed in the ultimate conquest. He sees it. His vision is clear. God shows it to him. But he doesn't possess it. Nevertheless, he is special. God loves him far too much to allow anyone else to bury him or even so much as attend his funeral. It is a scene of pathos that is bittersweet and unsurpassed. There, alone, steely-eyed and never flinching, God looks Moses in the eye as his life seeps from him. Moses knows God can save him, and waits. God never relents, shows no emotion, but continues His stoic and unrelenting gaze. Moses waits. God never blinks. No tears. No compromise. The eyes of Moses look pleadingly into God's face but to no avail. Moses dies never knowing how deeply God feels toward him, his beloved leader. The last breath leaves his body. He is gone. His journey ends on this lonely mount. But what do we now hear? The isolated, private, deep, heaving sobs of divine lament! Tell no man, but God weeps. With divine arms of affection, God slowly picks up the slack, exhausted body of His servant. With unspeakable emotion, He carries him to a secret, special burial place. There, in the solitude, He gently lowers the body. God tenderly lays him to rest. The Bible then says a strange thing. The writer declares:

"And there arose not a prophet since in Israel like unto Moses, whom the Lord knew face to face"
Deuteronomy 34:10

Knew face to face? What does this mean? Probably several things. However, some believe that this is God now looking into the tranquil face of His beloved servant. Now God quietly lowers Himself and carefully kneels beside him. Then, slowly bending forward, He looks into the now composed face of His beloved servant, and with a tearful tenderness only possible to divinity, God comes close...and ever so gently...kisses him. Kissed by God! And some thought that there was then a moaning of the wind. However, others thought it was a divine groan which said, "Oh my precious, precious Moses, soon I will awaken you and you shall see another who also will stand on a wilderness mount looking into the land...but nothing shall be able to stop Him."

Chapter 7

Sons of God and Adoption

We have seen that Sons of God are a product of special creation. It is to be sons by something apart from normal, natural birth. Just as the angels and Adam and Israel and Christ are special in birth and creation, so are we.

> "But to as many as did receive and welcome Him, He gave the authority (power, privilege, right) to become the children of God, that is, to those who believe in (adhere to, trust in, and rely on) His name—who owe their birth neither to bloods, nor to the will of the flesh [that of physical impulse] nor the will of man [that of a natural father], but to God. [They are born of God!]"
> John 1:12, 13 (Amp.)

What a glorious truth! Nothing on earth can match this. However, if we all, by being born of the Spirit (John 3:3, 5), are Sons of God, then should it not follow that all of us are automatically powerful ministers of the gospel? The answer to that is, in ideal terms, "Yes," all should, by the water and Spirit baptism, be powerful ministers of the gospel. And to the extent that we actualize that power within us, we do, indeed, experience commensurate effectiveness. To the extent that one's new birth Spirit baptism parallels Christ's empowerment at *baptism,* the answer is "Yes," one is so empowered at that point. That power is real. It is authentic and ready to be accessed upon demand. It is available to the newest believers.

On the other hand, to the extent that our spiritual birth in type parallels Christ's birth as a *baby,* then the answer is "No." In this parallel, to be born of the Spirit does not immediately mantle one with the same leadership ministry anointing as Christ experienced at His baptism. As the Son of God, and being conceived by the Holy Ghost, Christ obviously has the power of the Spirit in Him from birth. Likewise, all believers also have the power of the Spirit in them from the moment of spiritual birth. Just as Christ is the Son of God from birth, those born of water and spirit are also Sons (children) of God from spiritual birth. However, scripturally, in regards to leadership and to ministry, there is an important difference between being a son and being declared a son. It is this declaration which makes a radical difference. It is the declaration that activates the source of power and authority. In scripture, as well as in Jewish traditions, this declaration is designated as "adoption."

Adoption — The Transfer of Authority

We have examined the leadership model of Jesus as compared to Adam and Israel. What do we here see?

The fact that practically jumps out at us is the enormous concentrated opposition that is encountered at *the defining moment* in which God attempts to transfer authority to each of these chosen ones. There can be no doubt that this is the primary spiritual event instant for both Israel (who apparently has little awareness that their opposition is demonic in origin) as well as Christ. The goal of the enemy is to prevent God's chosen from obtaining and using the authority and power intended for them. God desired to give both Israel and Christ dominion—a dominion through which God Himself could bless mankind with liberty and righteous government. For this to happen, the present possessor of dominion, Satan, must surrender his hold. His refusal to do so simply underscores his rebellious and wicked nature. The process whereby God, as Father, transfers His authority to His Son, is adoption.

The term "adoption," as used in scripture, has more than one layer of meaning and varies somewhat from the term used in English. Strict English usage is simply that those who are not children by birth can become children of parents by a legal process called adoption. In contrast, Jewish usage, while permitting the above meaning, also includes the idea of a point in time in which a father deems his son old enough and responsible enough to have the same official authority as does his father in matters of the family household. The father determines when this time had arrived.

The arrival of the adoption time is a very, very important occasion in the life of a family household. Today, this is approximated in Jewish homes as the bar-mitzvah. The father announces that the time has come. Family and close friends gather. The son, who has come of age and who has found the favor of his father, is then placed in an elevated position for all to see. The father makes a solemn proclamation for all to hear and says something like, "This is my beloved son, in whom I am well pleased. From this day forward, he is to be recognized as having the authority to transact business and speak for this house. Hear ye him."

One might ask why the father declares him to be a son when all present are already aware that he is son. The answer to this is that this is not simply intended to inform everyone that this is his son, but rather, it is a legal declaration which indicates a transfer of power and of authority from the father of the household to the son. The son now has the power to speak in place of the father. His words are the father's words. All the authority of the house is his to exercise—and he is expected to responsibly exercise it to advance the father's interest.

The son does not have this power until this declaration. Though a son, his authority in the family is less than some servants. Hence, nothing is recorded of Jesus doing ministry prior to this declaration as He comes out of the waters of baptism. Prior to the declaration, He is under tutors and treated as a servant. Paul declares:

> *"Now I say, That the heir, as long as he is a child, differeth nothing from a servant, though he be Lord of all; But is under tutors and governors until the time appointed of the father. But when the fulness of the time was come, God sent forth his Son, made of a woman, made under the law."*   *Galatians 4:1, 2, 4*

Jesus is, indeed, the Son of God from birth. But this is not the same as being declared the Son of God with authority. Being son by birth immediately qualifies one for the inheritance of the Father (Romans 8:15,16). But being declared the Son of God with authority is a legal declaration of transfer of all the power invested in the family name (John 5:43). It is a position of responsibility and stewardship. Of this, Paul says:

> *"Concerning his Son Jesus Christ our Lord, which was made of the seed of David according to the flesh; And declared to be the Son of God with power (authority)..."*
> *Romans 1:3, 4*

Being son by birth from His mother's womb, He is "made" of the seed of David. But His power (authority) as Son comes only by **declaration.** There is a moment—a defining moment of transfer—that becomes the foundation for His entire ministry. This is a moment in which the authority of the Father is transferred to the Son.

Is there any way to escape the fact that such a moment of transfer exists? Further, is it possible to avoid the conclusion that this defining moment is key to the most powerful leadership in the world —a leadership which excels, leadership which penetrates far beyond all other kinds or levels of leadership, leadership which is world-impacting? Whether it be Jacob or Moses, Joseph or David, Elisha or Jonah, Jesus...or you, is there any escape from the terrible, wonderful, dreadful, glorious, revelatory, decisive moment of declaration and all that it entails? Is there true, world-class, apostolic ministry apart from such?

One may propose that Jesus has gone through all of that for us, hence, it is not for us to do so also. Our response is that perhaps this is so. Indeed, He has triumphed for us all. He paid this price, conquered Satan, and overcame the world, and on the cross emphatically declared, "It is finished."

Nevertheless, in terms of ministry, we know that the Christian life contains many parallels to the life of our Lord. In fact, the more one explores this fact, the more sobering it becomes. An example of this is seen in salvation. Our repentance is likened to His death. Our baptism is likened to His burial. And our new life in the Spirit is likened to His resurrection. Then, as already noted, Christ Himself declares that His leaders are sent as He is sent (John 17:18). Many concrete expressions in scripture validate that our ministry is not something apart from His ministry, but is an extension of Himself and His ministry. All of the above, coupled with the many additional biblical examples, reveal to us a consistent and unvarying template from which emerges the most powerful leadership in the world, that is, the reality of a decisive instant from which apostolic ministry emerges. The transfer of authority from the Father to His called and chosen ones is the key instant, the defining moment, from which springs genuine greatness. There are no shortcuts. There are no substitutes. God knows. The devil knows. Further, once they have been exposed to such ministry, the people also know.

This subject of Christ being declared the Son of God (Romans 1:3, 4) while often overlooked, is, nevertheless, very deeply embedded in scripture. Each succeeding declaration reinforces and adds to the authority and power of Christ's ministry. For example, that He has power even as a babe is witnessed by the power to draw angels, wise men, holy men (Simeon), holy women (Anna), and the kings. Further, at the age of twelve, His exceptional mental power and wisdom is seen. However, beyond the time of His birth by Mary, there are three such declarations of His Sonship and all of them include new and radical endorsements of power and authority. Each time they signal further movements in His ministry.

The first of these, as we have seen, is the formal declaration of His Sonship at baptism. *"This is my beloved Son, in whom I am well pleased"* (Matthew 3:17). We also observe how this propels Him into unprecedented power and authority to effect righteousness as a Heaven-anointed leader. The mantle of the Father's official transfer of power falls upon Him. Something dynamic beyond words transpires in Him. This seemingly innocuous life now explodes with divine power, authority, and energy. Luke reinforces this idea by virtually taking Christ straight from the temptation to Nazareth, where Christ immediately makes His debut as the Son who now acts as steward and authority of the Father's business on earth. Luke states:

> *"And He came to Nazareth, where he had been brought up: and, as his custom was, he went into the synagogue on the sabbath day, and stood up for to read...And when he had opened the book, he found the place where it was written, The Spirit of the Lord is upon me, because he hath anointed me to preach the gospel...to heal...to preach deliverance...to set at liberty them that are bruised, To preach the acceptable year of the Lord."*   *Luke 4:16-19*

The next time Christ is declared to be the Son of God is on the Mount of Transfiguration. And while not carrying the same degree of radical impact of the similar declaration at His baptism, there is nevertheless, a dramatic endowment which accompanies this event also. He is physically transfigured. He enters into conversation with Moses (here the two are again, on a high mountain at the center of God's eternal enterprise) and Elijah. Jesus converses with them of His impending death, signaling the next major phase of His ministry. Once again, His authority to complete the Father's mission is reinforced.

The first declaration of Christ's Sonship, at His baptism, initiates and sets the direction of His ministry. The second, on the Mount of Transfiguration, empowers His ministry for His death. The third and last such declaration is connected to Christ's resurrection. The last declaration of Christ's Sonship by the Father is the most far-reaching.

Beyond the above, there is another whole set of scriptures which we have not yet addressed, which deal precisely with sonship declarations by the Father this third time. The above two major declarations are primarily *verbal*. The third such declaration is primarily by *action*.

Psalm 2:7 is a prophetic utterance in which the Father says: "Thou art my Son; this day have I begotten thee" (or, "this day you have become my son"). Whatever this means, it has a powerful impact because in the next verse, revealing the empowerment He receives from this verse, God declares, "Ask of me, and I shall give thee the heathen for thine inheritance, and the uttermost parts of the earth for thy possession." Satan's temptation at Christ's baptism is a mimicry of this promise and therefore sounds eerily familiar. The following verse is even more emphatic in its declaration of authority and empowerment of the Son. *"Thou shalt break them with a rod of iron; thou shalt dash them in pieces like a potter's vessel"* (verse 9). The question is, When does He do this? He does this as a result of the declaration of Sonship in verse seven.

When was Psalm 2:7 fulfilled? Was it at Christ's baptism? On the Mount of Transfiguration? Or is this reference intended to neutralize the notion of eternal Sonship? The answer is none of the above.

The unquestionable authority in interpreting any Old Testament scripture is the New Testament. Thus, if the New Testament interprets the meaning and application of Psalm 2:7, we have our answer. Indeed, the correct application of this is found in Acts 13:33:

> *"God hath fulfilled the same unto their children, in that he hath raised up Jesus again; as it is also written in the second psalm, Thou art my Son, this day have I begotten thee."*

"Begotten" can also be translated as "born," or "this day have I become your father." What this means is not, of course, that Christ was naturally born again. It means, rather, that since Adam sinned, man has been dead to God. The Father/Son relationship which mankind had with God through Adam was severed at the Fall. Communion was destroyed. In the declaration, "This day I have begotten thee," He is speaking of the day Christ resurrected. By resurrecting to eternal life, the man Christ re-captured the Father/Son relationship which the first Adam lost, and reestablished the availability of communion with God for all men. Upon rising from the dead, the Father declares Christ's Sonship (i.e., His position and authority), and with it, the Sonship of all who are in Christ. Further, the resurrection now qualifies Christ for a new declaration of authority as the eternal High Priest of the human race. His "reward" is that God glorifies (empowers) Him to be this High Priest. He is "called of God" to be High Priest (Hebrews 5:10).

> *"So also Christ glorified not himself to be made an high priest; but He that said unto him, Thou art my Son, today have I begotten thee."*   Hebrews 5:5

He now stands on a mount higher than Moses' Nebo, higher than Satan's high place, higher than the Mount of Temptation. He stands on a mountain of ultimate victory. He has triumphed in battle and "the uttermost parts of the earth" are now His possession. He has also conquered the universe and all that is therein.

> *"(Now that he ascended, what is it but that he also descended first into the lower parts of the earth? He that descended is the same also that ascended up far above all heavens, that he might fill all things.) And what is the exceeding greatness of his power to usward who believe, according to the working of his mighty power, Which he wrought in Christ, when he raised him from the dead, and set him at his own right hand (i.e., place of authority) in the heavenly places, Far above all principality, and power, and might, and dominion, and every name that is named, not only in this world, but also in that which is to come."*
> *Ephesians 4:9,10; 1:19-22*

We, too, are declared to be God's sons (John 1:12). What, therefore, would cause one to think that the development pattern for leadership, deeply embedded in the Old Testament as well as in the New Testament, is going to vary when applied to today's ministry and call? Neither Christ nor Israel go directly from the call to the crowd. The battle is not first engaged with the visible, the public, and the concrete, but rather, with the spiritual, the unseen, and the shadowy. In this hostile, lonely landscape, experienced in the deep interior of the soul and in the world of spirit, hateful and malevolent forces are encountered, challenged and conquered, and the land of promise is captured.

In Christ's life, this declaration of Sonship (Romans 1:3,4) was God's call to ascending levels of ministry, authority, and responsibility. Do the demands of our call require a similar commitment to obedience? I believe the answer is "yes." Jesus was not a robot with no will. The call He experienced upon arising from baptism was real. Howbeit, He was not forced to go to the wilderness. He was not forced to wrestle out the issues of His ministry. Sensing the foreboding nature of the spiritual conflict before Him, His flesh most certainly shrank back from such.

What would have happened if, after the voice declared His authority and responsibility as the called, He had simply departed from the river scene and proceeded to go back to Rome? That is precisely what everyone else did, and God was evidently pleased with them. Would the anointing have been the same as recorded by Luke in chapter four verses 16-18? I think not. As applied to Christ, the above questions are only hypothetical. As applied to us, however, they are very real. For many have been, upon their call, similarly confronted to go deeper, but instead have shied away from the spiritual implications of such a call, choosing rather to scamper back to the shallow familiarity of everyday life. What, then, is the result of this failure to complete the spiritual processes of one's primary spiritual event instant? Had Christ failed, would He have known His own self and ministry? Would He have been able to identify the core issues? Might He have resorted to seeking signs to validate the Word rather than preaching the Word with signs following? Is it possible that the depth of His understanding of the conflict would have been insufficient and that He may have opted for seeing success at the expense of losing His ministry to the Father? Is it possible that any ministerial accomplishment which is not the outcome of this completed process will, on the scales of divine authentication, be found to be wood, hay, and stubble shrouded in a golden colored blanket? Again, these are not hypothetical questions as they apply to us.

Is there any way to have effective spiritual leadership while avoiding all that is included in the adoption process? Does the Father require acceptance of all that is entailed in being called and declared sons? Can we ignore the responsibility for decision-making, for judging, for guiding, for nurturing, for being stewards over His household? How about just letting me be a simple servant in the house? Unfortunately, declared sons cannot abdicate their role and responsibility. No story more emphatically underscores this than the Prodigal Son.

The dilemma of the Prodigal Son (Luke 15) clearly reveals this resistance. When the time arrives for this younger son to take on the responsibilities of sonship, it is just too much. Scripture clearly reveals the diligence, faithfulness, and apparent skill of his older brother upon whom these responsibilities seems to rest so easily. His older brother is so good, so pleasing to their father, that the younger one is totally intimidated. He has no self-confidence. He feels inadequate. He loves his father dearly, but knows he is not the first- born and does not feel he can live up to the expectations that come with acknowledgment and acceptance of sonship. As long as they were both young, under tutors, and without responsibility, it was tolerable. But now he has come of age. It cannot be long before the time will come which will impose the dreaded responsibility for administration and decision making. A wise wielding of the father's authority will be expected. Others have looked to this day all of their lives. But for this son, it is too much. Taking what is his and hating himself for disappointing his father, he flees the house in shame and embarrassment.

For the next several years, with abandon, he plunges into attempt after attempt to anesthetize his mind from the dreaded responsibility he has fled. Each loop of the downward spiral to destruction and ruin is filled with ever more desperate attempts to drown away "the call." He does not succeed. Somewhere, though at times ever so faint, the ringing of "the call" penetrates his drunken, drugged mind. It is as though he is fated. He cannot escape. Like Jacob of old, God finally wrestles him down. There, pinned by God in the mud of a pig pen, he realizes he has no choice but to give up and throw himself on the mercy of his father. Luke says he "comes to himself." The re-recognition of who he is and his proper place comes to him. He arises and begins the long journey back home.

Still, his mind races frantically for ways to dwell with the father while escaping the dreaded responsibility of sonship. Finally his mind hits on a plan! It is so simple! How could he have overlooked such an answer? Confident that his father is already disappointed in him, he can return as a servant. Thus, his father can "save face" and he, the shame-bearing son, can gain readmittance to the home while still escaping sonship responsibilities. At least it's worth a try.

Passing familiar landmarks, he makes his way back home. Filled with self-loathing, he is uncertain, tentative, and afraid. Surely the father will simply ignore such a one. But we know this is not so. It is significant that the father never pursued this wayward boy. In the same chapter (Luke 15), the shepherd pursues the lost sheep and the woman pursues the lost coin. But the father does not pursue the lost boy. For in the case of the sheep and the coin, they have value, but they are not sons and, therefore, their stories do not include the process of spiritual formation. In the case of the boy, the father knows that it is essential to allow whatever time and process is required to subdue the human will of a son who is running from the adoption (Galatians 4) of sonship with its attendant authority and responsibilities.

The fact that the father did not pursue the son should not be perceived as anger or lack of interest. It reflects, rather, the father's awareness that an individual's rebellion dies a slow, agonizing death. The process must not be truncated. There are no shortcuts. For the son to receive all the glories of the kingdoms by bowing to become servant is a temptation of satanic origin. To accept success without acceptance of full stewardship responsibilities is to fail the covenant test.

So the father waits with an aching heart. In his mind's eye, he follows the downward spiral of his son's frantic attempts to escape destiny. Somewhere in the distant dark fog of sin he loses him and can only continue to follow by the eye of faith. Each day he rises and meets the first rays of the rising sun with hand shading eyes, looking down that long, long road for the return of his beloved son. He understands his son's pain. His empathy futilely reaches out to embrace his wounded boy and bring him home. Morning after morning, he returns to the house disappointed.

Until one morning, peering intently into the distance, he sees a ragged figure trudging and stumbling slowly up the road. It can't be—but it is! He recognizes the gait, the slope of the shoulders, the set of the head. It is his son, and he knows what this means. The father in his wisdom knows the boy has, by virtue of his return, already passed the major test. Age is forgotten as he sprints down the drive toward his long lost son. With tears pressed back by the wind, a moan of love and yearning emits from his breast. He lunges, embracing his son, covering him with kisses, mumbling, "My son which was lost has returned." Oh, how much a father loves his son! It is a love that understands the struggles, the doubts, the fears, the failures.

Shock registers on the son's face as he experiences the degree of intensity of the father's love and compassion. His sense of unworthiness increases ten-fold as he recognizes this undeserved display of favor. He is overwhelmed by the judgment-free reception from such a wise, loving father. Nevertheless, he still does not forget his plan for escaping sonship responsibilities and so he declares, "I am no longer worthy to be called your son; just make me as one of your hired servants."

The father stops abruptly and pulls away, slowly shaking his head. As they make their way back to the house, the father explains, "No, son, you cannot come home as a servant. You are no longer a little boy. You are a capable man whom I will empower with all the tools to be a steward. A son cannot simply be a servant." Thus, arriving in the yard where the family and servants have now gathered, the father puts his arm around the son stating, "My son who was lost is found." He then solemnly carries out the long-delayed adoption process which promotes his son from being under servants to the place of authority. This is signified by the placing of the family robe of authority on his shoulders and the sacred signet ring carved with the family crest on his finger. Now anything he puts his stamp or signature upon is the same as if the father had stamped it. The son has truly come home, but only on the father's conditions and only after the complete breaking of all resistance to acceptance of the responsibilities of his call.

Sons cannot live in the father's house as servants. No doubt there are some who will disregard all of the above, for it is easy to point out that there are other applications of the story of the Prodigal Son. This is true. However, that is not the question here. The really important question is, what about you? Is God talking to you? Do you have a voice coming to you today—your voice ringing deep in the recesses of your spirit—saying, "Yes, in ministry, I am that prodigal. My will has resisted the adoption process that leads to spiritual formation."

How long was the Prodigal Son on his circular journey? No one knows. That is not the essence of the story. The story is about coming home. Man or woman, no amount of resistance will change the father's mind. Dodging God's will is a masquerade party to which people come in many different costumes. However, when all is said, there is no alternate route for doing God's will.

Can one avoid the process of spiritual adoption to leadership and still experience authentic apostolic ministry? This question applies not only to preaching but also to the spiritual formation of any individual seeking God's will for their life. The Bible seems to indicate that no, there is no such genuine leadership outside of this confrontation with one's self, one's call, and one's development of understanding of process. There is evidently no alternative route, yet acceptance of this experience is always met with resistance.

A striking, current-day example of an individual's confrontation with one's self and one's call is a woman named Mary Wilson. She is my wife. However, married or not, when it comes to these issues, one always stands completely alone before God.

Almost from the day we were married, my wife and I have been in ministry. For many years, she was the consummate preacher's wife. Bubbly, cheerful, effervescent and exciting, as well as a tremendous cook and homemaker, she fulfilled every "womanly" responsibility. We raised our two girls as I pastored and taught and preached. Always faithful to God, faithful in prayer, and an influential person, she was also a tremendous musician and singer. I was content to lead and she was content to allow me to do so, often stating, "You are the one called and anointed to pastor and lead. I am just your helper." Whether in good times or times of rejection, she was always totally loyal, totally supportive, totally ready to simply help.

Then one day, after 22 years of marriage, something happened. She was 40. Though still young and strong and beautiful, she would not be allowed to continue as in the past. God came calling. She was content, but He wasn't. Laying His hand upon her, He beckoned her and turned her life upside down. "I've got to talk to you," she said to me one day. Talk? We talk all the time. "No," she replied, "This is different. I must talk to you alone, without interruption." Getting in the car, we drove to a lonely spot in the park and turned off the engine. In the solitude, she brokenly explained that she wasn't sure what had happened, except she was aware that God was touching her and she could no longer continue as in the past. She was not unhappy nor had anything adverse occurred. She tearfully and simply explained that she knew that life as she had lived it was over. She was, at once, sober, alone, and afraid. She feared what she saw and what she felt. She feared what could happen, what others might think, and what failures could occur. She wrestled with the awareness that I could not go there for her, or even with her, for God's call is the most private, individual thing in the world. He is a jealous God. Without defense and nakedly vulnerable, we stand before Him to receive His orders. She attempted to cling to me, all the while knowing that it was impossible to do so. I knew this also. Having been there myself, I understood the fear, the sense of plunging into the dark, the hesitancy to proceed. I could only encourage her and assure her that, in conquering her interior fears, she was also conquering hostile principalities and powers wandering in desert places. She must go alone. Only raw courage and obedience would suffice. She would go. She did go. The seed must first fall into the ground, dying, and abiding alone. It is the only way. But the result is new life. Where one seed dwells alone, there arises a thousand-fold reproduction. It is no different with spiritual formation for great leadership. Out of my wife's profound surrender to the Father's will was birthed a new and spectacular ministry which has now, over the last sixteen years, reproduced itself in thousands of lives of every age and continues to do so. It has also served as a primary force in catapulting an entire congregation into new, positive, and very powerful vistas of growth and progress and which continues to redound and grow to the glory of God.

It was a defining moment, a primary spiritual event instant in the life of a young woman. The question that remains is what about you? Do you hear God's call to world-class leadership? Behind your day-to-day activities, does the "tap-tap" of His Spirit on your heart continue to beckon you to follow Him to a place alone?

Chapter 8

Water Baptism

The following is an important story about greatness:

"Then came to him the mother of Zebedee's children with her sons, worshipping him, and desiring a certain thing of him. And he said unto her, What wilt thou? She saith unto him, Grant that these my two sons may sit, the one on thy right hand, and the other on the left, in thy kingdom. But Jesus answered and said, Ye know not what ye ask. Are ye able to drink of the cup that I shall drink of, and to be baptized with the baptism that I am baptized with? They say unto him, We are able."

Matthew 20:20-22

Here is a blatant request for greatness. The bold request is made for dominion, recognition, prominence, and power. Jesus Himself confirms that the subject is, indeed, the attaining of "greatness" (verse 26). He does not condemn the desire, but reveals the path necessary to its attainment.

Observation has already been made concerning the fact that, in the journey to spiritual formation, one is plunged deeply into the core issues of life and death. It is a place of elemental sacredness, rudimentary reality. It is a deep, high, holy, and intimidating chamber indeed. To some, such a description will no doubt appear extreme and unwarranted. These tend toward a view of ministry as any other vocation for which one prepares in a practical, systematic way. One learns the basics, develops beginning skills, is schooled in correct processes and procedures, serves an apprenticeship, then launches into full-scale ministry. There is a place and need for such. However, this is not at the core of greatness in leadership. World-class leaders are not simply efficient technicians. While skills certainly matter, they are, nevertheless, not the ultimate point in question.

In seeking greatness, James and John are led to baptism and "drinking"–both again connected with water and, in the case of baptism, going down into the deep where there is death, darkness, and uncertainty. All believers are submerged into baptism's "watery grave." *"Therefore we are buried with him by baptism into death..."* (Romans 6: 4). We are further informed that it is precisely this act of being *"planted together in the likeness of His death"* (verse 5) that is the key to experiencing walking *"in newness of life"* (verse 4). The old man is "crucified" with Him. Baptism is a disposing of the old life. It is a removal, a negative, *"...that the body of sin might be destroyed..."* (verse 6). *"Now if we be dead with Christ, we believe that we shall also live with Him..."* (verse 8).

Thus, baptism is the believer's Red Sea. It is the dividing line between the old life and the new, a crisis between life and death. Coming to God is not, first and foremost, a gradual process, but a complete and total interruption of one's old life and a revolutionary birth into the new. Coming out of the water, the Spirit says, "This is my beloved child." From there, the process of discipleship proceeds into the wilderness for both Christ as well as Israel.

Just as the Red Sea typifies baptism, it is not the last "baptism" for Israel. There is another at Jordan. Although they are already "God's people," they are at Jordan, preparing to enter a new realm of dominion, authority, and responsibility. To do so, they must cross Jordan. As the Red Sea was a "deep" demarcation line between bondage and freedom, so Jordan is a "deep" demarcation line between general living and the primary spiritual event instant called by God and strongly led, or driven, into spiritual crisis and victory. Coming out of this experience, God will again say, "This is my beloved Son," but this time, it will carry not only the meaning of being a part of the family, but also of being a son with distinct responsibilities and powers, as well as distinct authority and power for leadership. This authority is not confined to Christ alone, but is given to all those who lead in His stead. The Lord reveals in His prayer, *"As thou has sent me into the world, even so have I also sent them into the world"* (John 17:18).

Sent as He is sent! He spoke not as the scribes and Pharisees, but rather, He spoke as One with authority! No academician here quoting first this opinion, then that. He speaks rather as an owner–an owner of truth and of the ground of absolute reality. Luke purposely arranges the events of the early ministry of Jesus to point to the cataclysmic baptism and subsequent wilderness temptation of Jesus as the clear turning point in His life. Coming out of this temptation, Luke presents Him as returning to Nazareth where He introduces His own ministry with:

> *"The spirit of the Lord is upon me because He hath anointed me to preach the gospel to the poor; He hath sent me to heal the broken-hearted, to preach deliverance to the captives, and recovering of sight to the blind, to set at liberty them that are bruised, to preach the acceptable year of the Lord"*
> *Luke 4:18, 19*

Upon reading Luke 3:21 through 4:19, one can hardly fail to see the connection between the baptism/wilderness experience and His experience of a new anointing for ministry. Thus, it is evident that the theological meaning of Christ's ministry begins at Jordan's baptism, not Bethlehem's birth.

Alone or Together?

The question arises, Does spiritual formation take place individually, in isolation, or does it develop primarily in the context of community? Is isolation where "real" spirituality is found, or does it reside in coexistence? Must one escape the grasp of others and flee to a place of spiritual formation or are "others" helpful in the process? Does this formation involve a "person and his God" or a "people and their God"? On which side does truth stand? Does the pendulum swing toward aloneness or togetherness?

The answer is that aloneness and togetherness are equally involved in spiritual formation. They are polar in nature. If one is lost, both are lost. It is a condition of finite existence to be pulled first by the need for individuality and then by the need for community. This will not change. Too much of one aspect creates a sense of need for the other. However, in terms of which comes first in the process of spiritual formation for leadership and ministry, it is clearly individualism.

It all begins with one's individual salvation, of which nothing is more personal. No relationship in life is more intimate, more private, more tender, or more precious than this private, internal, subjective birth and ensuing communion with the Savior. It is beyond words. Nothing is more defining of what is sacred, holy, and separate than this one-to-one relationship. The individual salvation event is, in itself, the greatest "leap of faith" in the lives of new converts. Leaving the old world behind, risking every other relationship they have ever known, laying every other aspect of their existence open to loss, and knowing that they will be misunderstood, new converts leap with abandon into the arms of Jesus through faith, obedience, and surrender. Walking down a long aisle, they willingly shed all that has ever meant anything to them to grasp Christ. Surely the power of the old rugged cross holds a wondrous attraction! What power, what authority, what magnetism it possesses! It defiantly flings down the gauntlet of allegiance in the face of every worldly passion, every human interest, every earthly invention. In contrast to all that seems rational and logical, caught in its entrancement, they rise from their seat of sin, never to return. New converts die out to their past life and leave it buried in the waters of baptism. Going down in the water as a son of Adam the First Man, they arise as a son of the last Adam, the Second Man. They are given a new name, a new family, and a new inheritance. When they receive the Holy Spirit, they are infused with a new source of life–not blood–but Spirit. Receiving the Holy Spirit is tantamount to having the resurrected Christ and the Spirit of the God of all creation residing within them–dwelling in a way that is mysterious beyond words, fusing humanity with divinity, finite with infinite, becoming one body and one spirit.

However, this individual nature of spiritual formation does not end with one's initial salvation. The disciplines of systematic private devotion, personal prayer and fasting, apart from any corporate forms of the same, are also very individual. All of these play a key role in developing a disciplined spiritual life of strength and character.

Isolation is not only inseparable from the new birth experience, but also from spiritual formation for leadership. God, as we have seen in the life of Jesus and others, brings His leader, with all of his or her latent potential, to an empowering moment of decision in which there is a ripping away of the veil that has hidden the demands of God upon his life. At this decisive moment, God reveals His purposes and depths to which He is going to empower the one called. The one called is thus exposed to the yawning deep of a universal struggle. Poised on the edge of a precipice, he sees the deep into which he is going to leap or be thrust. This is a time of extreme isolation, ultimate aloneness, and individual confrontation between one's self and the demonic world. It is the development of impacting ministry. However, there can be no impact without a collision. The person being developed collides with God's Will, his own will, and the will of the predictable flow of history, plus the stubbornness of powers hostile to both. This often transpires all at once. It is personally cataclysmic. Of all leadership moments, this is by far the most defining, the most traumatic, the most terror-ble.

The recipient of this encountering experience is never the same. One no longer finds fulfillment in banal conversation and superficial living, and thus experiences a restlessness and dissatisfaction with shallowness and a newfound authority over one's life. There is also a desire to connect with others like oneself who have traveled beyond anonymous existence into a world of meaning, purpose, and authenticity.

The phrase "anonymous existence" is a borrowed one. Philosophers have pictured man as hopelessly separated from the infinite which he can see but cannot reach. He thus dangles between the infinity of his aspirations and the finite limitations of his possibilities. Man is caught in a "desperate encounter between human inquiry and the silence of the universe" (Camus, 1954). The common populace deals with this by choosing anonymous existence, an existence that hides the impossibility of their situation behind the mask of mundane and daily concerns. Fearing the consequences of admitting that their existence is absurd, they gloss it over with exaggerated attendance to the inconsequential. Life is simply an anonymous existence.

These same philosophers take the position that co-existence with other people is a condemnation or alienation of man (Sartre) and is something to be escaped:

"When…you go striding down the long streets– Then for that evening you have completely got away from your family, which fades into insubstantiality, while you yourself, a firm, boldly drawn black figure, slapping yourself on the thigh, grow to your full stature."

Kafka, *The Sudden Walk*

This idea that one becomes greater who stands apart from others with a gentle disdain has received coinage not only in philosophy but also theologically through asceticism and other doctrines that have developed through the centuries. In conjunction with this position is the related idea that everybody is a nobody, and that nothing matters.

"I'd love to go on an excursion–why not?–with a pack of nobodies. Into the mountains, of course, where else? How these nobodies jostle each other, all these lifted arms linked together, these numberless feet treading so close…"

Kafka, *Excursion in the Mountains*

For those who have encountered God in the way described in this book, the result is diametrically opposed to the above philosophical conclusions. The universe is no longer silent. Man no longer dangles between the infinity of his aspirations and the finite limitations of his possibilities. His possibilities are no longer limited by finite conditions. He has come to "heavenly places" above such conditions. Co-existence with others is not a condemnation, nor is everyone "nobodies," but rather, every person has intrinsic worth, made in the image of God, regardless of environmental or sociological factors. Existence is no longer anonymous and obscure, but rather, is imbued with courage, clarity, and robust, transcendent purpose. Finally, there is an awareness that, although the overwhelming majority of the world does dwell in anonymous existence, there are those who do not. This group, while small, is critical to the hopes of mankind, for they are those who lead and who, through call and courage, have broken through the shell of anonymity and found identity. We call them leaders–God-anointed, empowered, aware leaders. While they may not have begun with more potential than others, they have "taken the leap," plunged headlong into the deep, "broken through," and adjusted to the rocking characteristic of life in a fluid environment.

The future of the church and the world is dependent upon this group. It has never been a large group. It is a small group of men and women with deep insight who have collaborated in a calling, the success of which is almost beyond belief. Peter, James, John, and the others are called by the Lord. In radical fashion, they leave their nets and follow. The tiny troupe who embrace this way of life are the soul of spiritual reality in the church and on the earth. If these falter or become subject to those who have no experience of the deep, the hope of spiritual life shrivels, and life moves back toward anonymous existence. The result is darkness and barbarism and a return to chaos.

Superficiality can neither found nor sustain worth. Both the church and the world are utterly dependent upon the deep thinking and living of those who have escaped anonymity. A community and world that are based on spiritual understanding must have leaders who are attuned to walking in the world of Spirit. Under the very best of times, there are only a few in any movement to gather, pray, exchange their understandings, and guide the young in the ways of the Kingdom. Direction comes to the lowest by awareness of the highest. When no one goes to the high to point the way, then no check remains to the egotistical tendency of thinking too highly of oneself. Leveled by the pervasive democratic idea of "equality," greatness and destiny become unwelcome. The result is that mediocre experiences, because they are not placed beside those of genuine worth, receive coinage far beyond their value. In this atmosphere, the notation that some are "born for this purpose," (i.e., to lead) is passed off as elitism and is replaced by the elitism of scorn. In such a society, all greatness is derived—none has the stamp of personal experience and power. When these finally succeed, they can hardly wait to remove the exhilarating mountain peaks of revelation and plunge all into an insipid spiritual soup of reductionist utilitarianism. The result is mediocrity energized by human hubris, which, when ascending into the sacred chambers of greatness, is doomed to be revealed to be wood, hay, and stubble.

True greatness has a connectedness that transcends time and place. Jesus connected to the Old Testament. Peter connected to Jesus. We connect to Jesus and with Peter. John the Baptist connected to Elijah so tightly that Jesus described him as Elijah. Jesus connected to Elijah and Moses at the same time! Elisha connected to Elijah. We connect to Elijah (e.g., James 5:17). Even more startling is the fact that the future is connected to Elijah, and to Jesus, etc. The communion table connects back "with His death" and forward "till He comes" (1Corinthians 11:26).

Greatness is always networked with greatness. Alexander slept with a copy of Achilles under his head. Napoleon tied the ancient dreams of Alexander to his own. It is said that when someone asked Boris Yeltsin where he obtained the courage to stand on a roof in defiance of the tanks of the crumbling communist regime of Russia and stare them down, he explained that he remembered the courage a few years earlier of Lech Walensa, a plumber in Poland who bravely stood before the mighty Polish communist regime and defied them until they folded. In turn, when Lech Walensa was asked where he got such courage, he responded that he saw the courage of Martin Luther King in the United States, who was willing to stand and lead regardless of risks. When Martin Luther King was asked from whence came his determination, he responded that he was inspired by Rosa Parks, the little, nondescript black lady from the Deep South who one day stepped out of anonymous existence and refused to give up her seat on the municipal bus, thus propelling forward the fall of segregation in America. Should we, then, give a great degree of credit to Rosa Parks for the global fall of Communism? In ways of which she could have never dreamed, her courage found its way onto the world stage. Her greatness in personal example escaped the confines of the bus upon which she rode and was "released into the atmosphere," caught by the winds of current events, and carried outward to become a change agent in the world on a scale that no one could have foreseen.

This is the way of authentic leadership. It is indiscriminate. When "right" is done in secret, it is rewarded openly by the Father who seeth in secret. As with Rosa Parks, courage to do right in a small situation often escapes the situation and reflects itself boldly on the canvas of much larger stages. Doing right transcends immediacy. Like Atticus in "To Kill a Mockingbird," right "outs" regardless of the verdict of its immediate surroundings. Though the setting in which it is released may be small, there is no small courage, righteousness, or honesty.

We speak here not of the nit-picky, power-grabbing, ego-driven, self-aggrandizing pursuit of position, personal advantage, or personal notice. At least five times in Matthew chapter six, Jesus cautions about doing things "to be seen of men." In contrast, authentic leaders possess an authority that is borne of white-hot passion for God, for people, for justice, for freedom, and for righteousness. They connect in ways in which all the corrupt power-brokers in the world can never duplicate or prevent. Neither time nor walls have the power to stop such. The spirits of great leaders find each other, and a small but highly concentrated fellowship is born. Race, color, gender, economics, appearance, favored status—none of these matter in this arena.

Spiritual leaders on the highest level realize that there is an ongoing "conversation of the ages"–a conversation that transcends time, space, and the here and now (see Hebrews 12:22-25). Christ speaks to Moses and Elijah. Joel's voice carries over centuries and speaks to Peter at Pentecost, who, in turn, speaks to his present time and place a message so fresh and powerful as to open dramatic new vistas heretofore inexperienced. The synergistic effect of the continued fellowship of greatness through the centuries creates a tremendous field of energy and power. Finding each other are those who penetrate deeply into the meaning of the gospel and the purposes of God. These are men and women who have taken the leap, gone "over the edge," plunged far into the deep, and sailed into the foreboding. These are men and women whose calls have been honed on the mountain and fired in the desert in face-to-face confrontations with the most powerful anti-God forces in the universe, encountering their fetid breath and feeling the slime and filth and brutality of their nature, yet without giving ground. They have applied themselves to thorough and repeated heart purifications. They have studied long, prayed hard, dared greatly, expanded their horizons, stayed consistent in their pursuit, and developed an understanding and appreciation for the richness and breadth and depth of the Kingdom of God. They have given much, disregarded sacrifice, and brought hope to the oppressed. Their beliefs are convictions–something far beyond the pale of opinions. They have learned to appreciate the fellowship of the small band of fellow-travelers who are likewise. The place to which they have come is a great and glorious one. Their work is no longer work, but a grand cosmic adventure and an honor before which they humbly and silently bow and gratefully cast their talents, abilities, and energies. Imbued with the other-worldly, they obtain a sacred respect for the holy...and perhaps a little disdain for the casuistry of those who count the cost and shrink away, cowering in self-will and terror before the challenge of "becoming." Giving no quarter, God himself issues the old challenge for our new day:

> *"Gird up thy loins now like a man: I will demand of thee, and declare thou unto me."*
>
> *Job 40:7*

Bibliography

Anderson, R., *Theological Foundations for Ministry: Selected Readings for a Theology of the Church in Ministry.* Eardmans, Grand Rapids, Michigan, 1978.

Camus, A., *The Rebel,* Vintage Books, New York, NY, 1954.

Fenton, F., *The Holy Bible in Modern English,* A.C. Black, London, (1944 reprint of the 1910 edition)

Gaebelein, F.E., Ed. *The Expositor's Bible Commentary,* Zondervan Publishing House, Grand Rapids, MI, 1990.

Harris, R.W., Ed., *The New Testament Greek-English Dictionary,* The Complete Biblical Library, Springfield, MO, 1990.

Kafka, F., *Collected Stories,* Alfred A. Knopf, Publisher, New York, NY, 1993.

Kaiser, W. C., *Toward an Old Testament Theology,* Zondervan Publishing House, Grand Rapids, MI, 1978.

Ladd, G. E., *Jesus and the Kingdom,* Harper & Row Publishers, New York, N.Y., 1964.

Mauser, U.W., *Christ in the Wilderness,* A.R. Allenson, Inc., Naperville, IL, 1963.

Nouwen, H., *The Wounded Healer,* Doubleday & Company, Inc., Garden City, N.Y., 1972.

Patai, R., *The Children of Noah: Jewish Seafaring in Ancient Times,* Princeton University Press, Princeton, New Jersey, 1998.

Pedersen, J., *Israel,* Publisher unknown, 1926. Schroeder, G.L. *The Science of God,* Broadway Books, New York, NY, 1997.

Sweet, L., *Aqua Church,* Group Publishing, Inc., Loveland, CO, 1999.

Weymouth, R.F., *The New Testament in Modern Speech,* Revised by J.A. Robertson. James Clarke and Co. Ltd. and Harper and Row Publishers, Inc., London, 1908.

Wheatley, M.J. & Kellner-Rogers, M., *A Simpler Way,* Berrett-Koehler Publishers, San Francisco, CA, 1996

Wilson, N. J., *Plain Talk about the Man of God & His Work.* Reach Ministries, Hazelwood, MO, 1981.

Yancey, P. , *"Beyond Flesh and Blood,"* Christianity Today, 4/02/2001.